The Construction of
Social Reality

THE FREE PRESS

New York London Toronto Sydney Tokyo Singapore

John R. Searle

The Construction
of Social Reality

The Free Press
A Division of Simon & Schuster Inc.
1230 Avenue of the Americas, New York, N.Y. 10020

Printed in the United States of America

printing number

  2 3 4 5 6 7 8 9 10

Library of Congress Cataloging-in-Publication Data

Searle, John R.
    The construction of social reality / John R. Searle.
      p.   cm.
    Includes bibliographical references.
    ISBN 0–02–928045–1
    1. Social epistemology.   2. Philosophy of mind.   I. Title.
  BD175.S43   1995   94–41402
  121—dc20   CIP

For Dagmar

Contents

Acknowledgments

The first version of these ideas was presented as the Immanuel Kant lectures in Stanford in 1992. Subsequent versions were presented as the Thalheimer Lectures at Johns Hopkins, the Hempel lectures at Princeton, and as a series of lectures at the College de France in Paris. I have also presented this material in seminars in Berkeley and at the University of Graz in Austria. Several of my colleagues read parts of the manuscript and made helpful criticisms. Special thanks are due to Kent Bach, Martin Jones, Lisa Lloyd, Brian McLaughlin, Stephen Neale, and Neil Smelser.

In addition to the lecture series and university courses just mentioned, I have also had the opportunity to try out some of these ideas in several universities in the United States and Europe. We often hear how dreadful contemporary intellectual life is, but I have to say from my own experience that one of the great pleasures of the present era is that one can go just about anywhere in the world and lecture, in English, to audiences that are sympathetic, intelligent, helpful and sophisticated in analytic philosophy. I cannot exaggerate the extent to which I have benefited from the comments of students, friends, colleagues, and total strangers. I really can't thank all of the people who made helpful comments, simply because I do not remember all of them. Among those I do remember, I am especially grateful to Pierre Bourdieu, Herman Capellen, Hubert Dreyfus, Gilbert Harman,

Robert Harnish, Meleana Isaacs, Saul Kripke, Francois Recanati, David Sosa, and Charles Spinosa.

For exceptional hospitality during the course of writing this book, I am grateful to Ann and Gordon Getty and Drue Heinz. Thanks are also due to the entire passenger list of the *Midnight Saga* and the *Rosenkavalier* for putting up so graciously with my relentless pounding on the computer.

Special thanks to my research assistant, Jennifer Hudin, who was helpful at every step of the way, from the earliest formulation of the basic ideas to the final preparation of the index. As always my greatest debts are to my wife, Dagmar Searle, to whom this book is dedicated.

Introduction

We live in exactly one world, not two or three or seventeen. As far as we currently know, the most fundamental features of that world are as described by physics, chemistry, and the other natural sciences. But the existence of phenomena that are not in any obvious way physical or chemical gives rise to puzzlement. How, for example, can there be states of consciousness or meaningful speech acts as parts of the physical world? Many of the philosophical problems that most interest me have to do with how the various parts of the world relate to each other—how does it all hang together?—and much of my work in philosophy has been addressed to these questions. The theory of speech acts is in part an attempt to answer the question, How do we get from the physics of utterances to meaningful speech acts performed by speakers and writers? The theory of the mind I have attempted to develop is in large part an attempt to answer the question, How does a mental reality, a world of consciousness, intentionality, and other mental phenomena, fit into a world consisting entirely of physical particles in fields of force? This book extends the investigation to social reality: How can there be an objective world of money, property, marriage, governments, elections, football games, cocktail parties and law courts in a world that consists entirely of physical particles in fields of force, and in which some of these particles are organized into systems that are conscious biological beasts, such as ourselves?

Because these questions concern what might be thought of as problems in the foundations of the social sciences, one might suppose that they would have been addressed and solved already in the various social sciences, and in particular by the great founders of the social sciences in the nineteenth century and the early parts of the twentieth century. I am certainly no expert on this literature, but as far as I can tell, the questions I am addressing in this book have not been satisfactorily answered in the social sciences. We are much in debt to the great philosopher-sociologists of the nineteenth and early twentieth centuries—one thinks especially of Weber, Simmel, and Durkheim—but from such acquaintance with their works as I have, it seems to me that they were not in a position to answer the questions that puzzle me, because they did not have the necessary tools. That is, through no fault of their own, they lacked an adequate theory of speech acts, of performatives, of intentionality, of collective intentionality, of rule-governed behavior, etc. This book is an attempt to answer a set of traditional questions using resources that I and others have developed while working on other related questions.

A word about the organization of the book. The main argument is in the first half, Chapters 1 through 5. In these chapters I attempt to develop a general theory of the ontology of social facts and social institutions. The main question is, How do we construct an objective social reality? I apologize for a certain amount of repetition in these chapters, but in the nature of the case I was forced to go over and over the same ground to try to make sure I was getting it right. In Chapter 6 I try to locate the explanatory force of the constitutive rules of human instititions, given the puzzling fact that the agents in question are typically unconscious of the rules. To do that I have to explain my notion of the "Background" of nonconscious nonrepresentational capacities and abilities that enable us to cope with the world. In early drafts of the book I devoted an initial chapter to defending realism, the idea that there is a real world independent of our thought and talk, and to defending the correspondence conception of truth, the idea that our true statements are typically made true by how things are in the real world that exists independently of the statements. I think that realism and a correspondence conception are essential presuppositions of any sane philosophy, not to mention of any science, and I wanted to make clear some of my reasons for thinking so. But what was originally intended as fairly short introductory material developed a life of its own, as is usually the case with such large philosophical questions. When the first chapter grew to three I decided to move all of this material to the back of the book, lest it overbalance my main argument. Chapters 7 and 8 are discussions of realism, Chapter 9 is a defense of a version of the correspondence conception of truth.

1

The Building Blocks
of Social Reality

The Metaphysical Burden of Social Reality

This book is about a problem that has puzzled me for a long time: there are portions of the real world, objective facts in the world, that are only facts by human agreement. In a sense there are things that exist only because we believe them to exist. I am thinking of things like money, property, governments, and marriages. Yet many facts regarding these things are "objective" facts in the sense that they are not a matter of your or my preferences, evaluations, or moral attitudes. I am thinking of such facts as that I am a citizen of the United States, that the piece of paper in my pocket is a five dollar bill, that my younger sister got married on December 14, that I own a piece of property in Berkeley, and that the New York Giants won the 1991 superbowl. These contrast with such

1

facts as that Mount Everest has snow and ice near the summit or that hydrogen atoms have one electron, which are facts totally independent of any human opinions. Years ago I baptized some of the facts dependent on human agreement as "institutional facts," in contrast to noninstitutional, or "brute," facts.[1] Institutional facts are so called because they require human institutions for their existence. In order that this piece of paper should be a five dollar bill, for example, there has to be the human institution of money. Brute facts require no human institutions for their existence. Of course, in order to *state* a brute fact we require the institution of language, but the *fact stated* needs to be distinguished from the *statement* of it.

The question that has puzzled me is, How are institutional facts possible? And what exactly is the structure of such facts? But in the intervening years some curious things have happened. Many people, including even a few whose opinions I respect, have argued that all of reality is somehow a human creation, that there are no brute facts, but only facts dependent on the human mind. Furthermore, several people have argued against our common-sense idea that there are facts in the world that make our statements true and that statements are true because they correspond to the facts. So after attempting to answer my original question, How is a socially constructed reality possible? I want also to defend the contrast on which the question rests. I want to defend the idea that there is a reality that is totally independent of us (Chapters 7 and 8). Furthermore, because my method of investigation is to examine the structure of the facts that make our statements true and to which they correspond when they are true, I will also defend (a version of) the correspondence theory of truth (Chapter 9). The last three chapters, therefore, are concerned with defending certain general assumptions about reality, representation, knowledge, and truth.

Some of the questions I am trying to answer in the main argument of the book (Chapters 1–6) are, How can there be an objective reality that exists in part by human agreement? For example, how can it be a completely objective fact that the bits of paper in my pocket are money, if something is money only because we believe it is money? And what is the role of language in constituting such facts?

To give you a feel for the complexity of the problem, I want to begin by considering the metaphysics of ordinary social relations. Consider a simple scene like the following. I go into a café in Paris and sit in a chair at a table. The waiter comes and I utter a fragment of a French sentence. I say, *"un demi, Munich, à pression, s'il vous plaît."* The waiter brings the beer and I drink it. I leave some money on the table and leave. An innocent scene, but its metaphysical complexity is truly staggering, and its complexity would have taken Kant's breath away if he had ever bothered to think about such things.* Notice that we cannot capture the features of the description I have just given in the language of physics and chemistry. There is no physical-chemical description adequate to define "restaurant," "waiter," "sentence of French," "money," or even "chair" and "table," even though all restaurants, waiters, sentences of French, money, and chairs and tables are physical phenomena. Notice, furthermore, that the scene as described has a huge, invisible ontology: the waiter did not actually own the beer he gave me, but he is employed by the restaurant, which owned it. The restaurant is required to post a list of the prices of all the *boissons,* and even if I never see such a list, I am required to pay only the listed price. The owner of the restaurant is licensed by the French government to operate it. As such, he is subject to a thousand rules and regulations I know nothing about. I am entitled to be there in the first place only because I am a citizen of the United States, the bearer of a valid passport, and I have entered France legally.

---

*Kant did not bother to think about such things because in his era philosophers were obsessed with knowledge. Much later, for a brief, glorious moment, they were obsessed with language. Now this philosopher at least is obsessed with certain general structural features of human culture.

Notice, furthermore, that though my description was intended to be as neutral as possible, the vocabulary automatically introduces normative criteria of assessment. Waiters can be competent or incompetent, honest or dishonest, rude or polite. Beer can be sour, flat, tasty, too warm, or simply delicious. Restaurants can be elegant, ugly, refined, vulgar, or out of fashion, and so on with the chairs and tables, the money, and the French phrases.

If, after leaving the restaurant, I then go to listen to a lecture or attend a party, the size of the metaphysical burden I am carrying only increases; and one sometimes wonders how anyone can bear it.

The Invisible Structure of Social Reality

One reason we can bear the burden is that the complex structure of social reality is, so to speak, weightless and invisible. The child is brought up in a culture where he or she simply takes social reality for granted. We learn to perceive and use cars, bathtubs, houses, money, restaurants, and schools without reflecting on the special features of their ontology and without being aware that they have a special ontology. They seem as natural to us as stones and water and trees. Indeed, if anything, in most cases it is harder to see objects as just natural phenomena, stripped of their functional roles, than it is to see our surroundings in terms of their socially defined functions. So children learn to see moving cars, dollar bills, and full bathtubs; and it is only by force of abstraction that they can see these as masses of metal in linear trajectories, cellulose fibers with green and gray stains, or enamel-covered iron concavities containing water.

The complex ontology seems simple; the simple ontology seems difficult. This is because social reality is created by us for our purposes and seems as readily intelligible to us as those purposes themselves. Cars are for driving; dollars for earning, spending, and saving; bathtubs for taking a bath. But once there is no function, no answer to the question, What's it for? we are left with a harder intellectual task of identifying things in terms of their intrinsic features without reference to our interests, purposes, and goals.

The invisibility of the structure of social reality also creates a problem for the analyst. We cannot just describe how it seems to us from an internal "phenomenological" point of view, because money, property, marriages, lawyers, and bathtubs do not seem to have a complex structure. They just are what they are, or so it seems. Nor can we describe them from the external behaviorist point of view, because the description of the overt behavior of people dealing with money, property, etc., misses the underlying structures that make the behavior possible. Nor, in turn, can we describe those structures as sets of unconscious computational rules, as is done by contemporary cognitive science and linguistics, because it is incoherent to postulate an unconscious following of rules that is inaccessible in principle to consciousness. And besides, computation is one of those observer-relative, functional phenomena we are seeking to explain.[2]

If neither the internal phenomenological nor the external behaviorist point of view is adequate, what then is the correct stance, the correct methodology, for describing the *structure* of social reality? To start with, in this chapter and the next, I will use a first-person intentionalistic vocabulary to try to lay bare certain elementary features of social ontology. Later, in Chapter 6, I will show how some, though not all, of the intentionalistic apparatus can be explained in terms of, and ultimately eliminated in favor of, what I have elsewhere called the "Background" of capacities, abilities, tendencies, and dispositions.

Fundamental Ontology

Since our investigation is ontological, i.e., about how social facts exist, we need to figure out how social reality fits into our overall ontology, i.e., how the existence of social facts relates to other things that exist. We will have to make some substantive presuppositions about *how the world is in fact* in order that we can even pose the questions we are trying to answer. We will be talking about how social reality fits into a larger ontology, but in order to do that, we will have to describe some of the features of that larger ontology.

The truth is, for us, most of our metaphysics is derived from physics (including the other natural sciences). Many features of the contemporary natural science conception of reality are still in dispute and still problematic. For example, one might think that the Big Bang Theory of the origin of the universe is by no means well substantiated. But two features of our conception of reality are not up for grabs. They are not, so to speak, optional for us as citizens of the late twentieth and early twenty-first century. It is a condition of your being an educated person in our era that you are apprised of these two theories: the atomic theory of matter and the evolutionary theory of biology.

The picture of reality derived from these two theories, to state it very crudely, is as follows: The world consists entirely of entities that we find it convenient, though not entirely accurate, to describe as particles. These particles exist in fields of force, and are organized into systems. The boundaries of systems are set by causal relations. Examples of systems are mountains, planets, H_2O molecules, rivers, crystals, and babies. Some of these systems are living systems; and on our little earth, the living systems contain a lot of carbon-based molecules, and make a very heavy use of hydrogen, nitrogen, and oxygen. Types of living systems evolve through natural selection, and some of them have evolved certain sorts of cellular structures, specifically, nervous systems capable of causing and sustaining consciousness. Consciousness is a biological, and therefore physical, though of course also mental, feature of certain higher-level nervous systems, such as human brains and a large number of different types of animal brains.

With consciousness comes intentionality, the capacity of the mind to represent objects and states of affairs in the world other than itself.* Not all consciousness is intentional, and not all intentionality is conscious. There are, for example, forms of consciousness such as undirected anxiety that do not represent anything; and there are many forms of unconscious intentionality, such as my belief, even when I am not thinking about it, that Bill Clinton is president. However, though there is no necessary connection between being an intentional state at a given time and being conscious then and there, nonetheless, there is an important necessary connection between the two, in that every intentional state that is unconscious is at least accessible to consciousness. It is the sort of thing that could be conscious. An unconscious intentional state has to be in principle accessible to consciousness.

Here, then, are the bare bones of our ontology: We live in a world made up entirely of physical particles in fields of force. Some of these are organized into systems. Some of these systems are living systems and some of these living systems have evolved consciousness. With consciousness comes intentionality, the capacity of the organism to represent objects and states of affairs in the world to itself. Now the question is, how can we account for the existence of social facts within that ontology?

Objectivity and Our Contemporary World View

Much of our world view depends on our concept of objectivity and the contrast between the objective and the subjective. Famously, the distinction is a matter of degree, but it is less often re-

---

*I use "intentionality" as a technical term meaning that feature of representations by which they are *about* something or *directed at* something. Beliefs and desires are intentional in this sense because to have a belief or desire we have to believe that such and such is the case or desire that such and such be the case. Intentionality, so defined, has no special connection with intending. Intending, for example, to go to the movies is just one kind of intentionality among others. For a fuller account of intentionality, see J. R. Searle, *Intentionality: An Essay in the Philosophy of Mind* (Cambridge: Cambridge University Press, 1983).

marked that both "objective" and "subjective" have several different senses. For our present discussion two senses are crucial, an
epistemic sense of the objective-subjective distinction and an *ontological* sense. Epistemically speaking, "objective" and "subjective" are primarily predicates of judgments. We often speak of
judgments as being "subjective" when we mean that their truth or
falsity cannot be settled "objectively," because the truth or falsity is
not a simple matter of fact but depends on certain attitudes, feelings, and points of view of the makers and the hearers of the judgment. An example of such a judgment might be, "Rembrandt is a
better artist than Rubens." In this sense of "subjective," we contrast such subjective judgments with objective judgments, such as
the judgment "Rembrandt lived in Amsterdam during the year
1632." For such objective judgments, the facts in the world that
make them true or false are independent of anybody's attitudes or
feelings about them. In this epistemic sense we can speak not only
of *objective judgments* but of *objective facts.* Corresponding to objectively true judgments there are objective facts. It should be obvious from these examples that the contrast between epistemic
objectivity and epistemic subjectivity is a matter of degree.

In addition to the *epistemic* sense of the objective-subjective
distinction, there is also a related *ontological* sense. In the ontological sense, "objective" and "subjective" are predicates of entities
and types of entities, and they ascribe modes of existence. In the
ontological sense, pains are subjective entities, because their
mode of existence depends on being felt by subjects. But mountains, for example, in contrast to pains, are ontologically objective
because their mode of existence is independent of any perceiver
or any mental state.

We can see the distinction between the distinctions clearly if we
reflect on the fact that we can make epistemically subjective statements about entities that are ontologically objective, and similarly,
we can make epistemically objective statements about entities that
are ontologically subjective. For example, the statement "Mt. Everest is more beautiful than Mt. Whitney" is about ontologically ob-

jective entities, but makes a subjective judgment about them. On the other hand, the statement "I now have a pain in my lower back" reports an epistemically objective fact in the sense that it is made true by the existence of an actual fact that is not dependent on any stance, attitudes, or opinions of observers. However, the phenomenon itself, the actual pain, has a subjective mode of existence.

The Distinction Between Intrinsic and Observer-Relative Features of the World

Historically in our intellectual tradition we make great distinctions between mind and body and between nature and culture. In the section on Fundamental Ontology, I tacitly abandoned the traditional dualistic conception of the relation of mind and body in favor of the view that the mind is just a set of higher-level features of the brain, a set of features that are at once "mental" and "physical." We will use the "mental," so construed, to show how "culture" is constructed out of "nature." The first step is to introduce a more fundamental distinction than those mentioned above. This is the distinction between those features of the world that exist independently of us and those that are dependent on us for their existence.

　　The features of the world I described in characterizing our fundamental ontology, e.g., mountains and molecules, exist independently of our representations of them. However, when we begin to specify further features of the world we discover that there is a distinction between those features that we might call *intrinsic* to nature and those features that exist *relative to the intentionality of observers, users, etc.* It is, for example, an intrinsic feature of the object in front of me that it has a certain mass and a certain chemical composition. It is made partly of wood, the cells of which are composed of cellulose fibers, and also partly of metal, which is itself composed of metal alloy molecules. All these features are intrinsic. But it is also true to say of the very same object that it is a screwdriver. When I describe it as a screwdriver, I am specifying a feature of the object that is observer or user relative. It is a screwdriver only because people use it as (or made it for the purpose of, or regard it as) a screwdriver. The existence of observer-relative features of the world does not add any new material objects to reality, but it can add epistemically objective *features* to reality where the features in question exist relative to observers and users. It is, for example, an epistemically objective feature of this thing that it is a screwdriver, but that feature exists only relative to observers and users, and so the feature is ontologically subjective. By "observers and users" I mean to include makers, designers, owners, buyers, sellers, and anyone else whose intentionality toward the object is such that he or she regards it as a screwdriver.

Since the issues are important and the example is simple, I want to belabor these points a bit further.

1. The sheer existence of the physical object in front of me does not depend on any attitudes we may take toward it.

2. It has many features that are intrinsic in the sense that they do not depend on any attitudes of observers or users. For example, it has a certain mass and a certain chemical composition.

3. It has other features that exist only relative to the intentionality of agents. For example, it is a screwdriver. To have a general term, I will call such features "observer relative." Observer-relative features are ontologically subjective.

4. Some of these ontologically subjective features are epistemically objective. For example, it isn't just my opinion or evaluation that it is a screwdriver. It is a matter of objectively ascertainable fact that it is a screwdriver.

5. Although the feature of being a screwdriver is observer relative, the feature of thinking that something is a screwdriver (treating it as a screwdriver, using it as a screwdriver, etc.) is intrinsic to the thinkers (treaters, users, etc.). Being a screwdriver is ob-

server relative, but the features of the observers that enable them to create such observer-relative features of the world are intrinsic features of the observers. I will shortly explain this point further.

It is not always immediately obvious whether a feature is intrinsic or observer relative. Colors are a good example. Prior to the development of physics in the seventeenth century, people thought of colors as intrinsic features of the world. Since then many people have come to think of them as properties that exist only relative to observers. It is intrinsic that light differentially scatters when reflected from surfaces, and intrinsic to people that they have subjective color experiences caused by the impact of light on their visual systems. But the further attribution of color properties to objects in the world is observer relative, because it can be made only relative to the experiences of observers, as caused by the impact of light. I am not here trying to settle the issue about colors, but calling attention to the fact that whether a feature is intrinsic or observer relative is not always obvious.

A good rough-and-ready way of getting at this distinction is to ask youself, Could the feature exist if there had never been any human beings or other sorts of sentient beings? Observer-relative features exist only relative to the attitudes of observers. Intrinsic features don't give a damn about observers and exist independently of observers. One qualification has to be added immediately to this test, and it is stated in point 5 above, namely, that acts of observing and using are themselves intrinsic. So, to put it very crudely, something is a screwdriver only relative to the fact that conscious agents regard it as a screwdriver; but the fact that conscious agents have that attitude is itself an intrinsic feature of the conscious agents. Because mental states, both conscious and unconscious, are themselves intrinsic features of the world, it is not strictly speaking correct to say that the way to discover the intrinsic features of the world is to subtract all the mental states from it. We need to reformulate our explanation of the distinction to account for this exception as follows: Intrinsic features of reality are those that exist independently of all mental states, except for mental states themselves, which are also intrinsic features of reality.

From a God's-eye view, from outside the world, all the features of the world would be intrinsic, including intrinsic relational features such as the feature that people in our culture regard such and such objects as screwdrivers. God could not see screwdrivers, cars, bathtubs, etc., because intrinsically speaking there are no such things. Rather, God would see *us treating* certain objects as screwdrivers, cars, bathtubs, etc. But from our standpoint, the standpoint of beings who are not gods but are inside the world that includes us as active agents, we need to distinguish those true statements we make that attribute features to the world that exist quite independently of any attitude or stance we take, and those statements that attribute features that exist only relative to our interests, attitudes, stances, purposes, etc.

In each of the following pairs, the first states an *intrinsic* fact about an object, and the second states an *observer-relative* fact about the very same object.

1a. intrinsic: That object is a stone.

1b. observer relative: That object is a paperweight.

2a. intrinsic: The moon causes the tides.

2b. observer relative: The moon is beautiful tonight.

3a. intrinsic: Earthquakes often occur where tectonic plates meet.

3b. observer relative: Earthquakes are bad for real estate values.

I want this distinction to seem quite obvious, because it is going to turn out that social reality in general can be understood only in light of the distinction. Observer-relative features are always created by the intrinsic mental phenomena of the users, observers, etc., of the objects in question. Those mental phenomena are, like all mental phenomena, ontologically subjective; and the observer-relative features inherit that ontological subjectivity. But this ontological subjectivity does not prevent claims about observer-relative features from being epistemically objective. Notice that in 1b and 3b the observer-relative statement is epistemically objective; in 2b it is subjective. These points illustrate the ways in which all three distinctions cut across each other: the distinction between the intrinsic and the observer relative, the distinction between ontological objectivity and subjectivity, and the distinction between epistemic objectivity and subjectivity.

It is a logical consequence of the account of the distinction as I have so far given it that for any observer-relative feature F, *seeming to be F* is logically prior to *being F*, because—appropriately understood—seeming to be F is a necessary condition of being F. If we understand this point, we are well on the road to understanding the ontology of socially created reality.

The Assignment of Function

My main objective in this chapter is to assemble the apparatus necessary to account for social reality within our overall scientific ontology. This requires exactly three elements. The assignment of function, collective intentionality, and constitutive rules. (Later, in Chapter 6, to explain the causal functioning of institutional structures, we will introduce a fourth element, the Background of capacities that humans have for coping with their environment.) In explaining these notions I am perforce in a kind of hermeneutic circle. I have to use institutional facts to explain institutional facts; I have to use rules to explain rules, and language to explain language. But the problem is expository and not logical. In the exposition of the theory I rely on the reader's understanding of the phenomena to be explained. But in the actual explanation given, there is no circularity.

The first piece of theoretical apparatus I need I will call the "assignment (or imposition) of function." To explain this, I begin by noting the remarkable capacity that humans and some other animals have to impose functions on objects, both naturally occurring objects and those created especially to perform the assigned functions.

As far as our normal experiences of the inanimate parts of the world are concerned, we do not experience things *as* material objects, much less as collections of molecules. Rather, we experience a world of chairs and tables, houses and cars, lecture halls, pictures, streets, gardens, houses, and so forth. Now all the terms I have just used involve criteria of assessment that are internal to the phenomena in question under these descriptions, but not internal to the entities under the description "material object." Even natural phenomena, such as rivers and trees, can be assigned functions, and thus assessed as good or bad, depending on what functions we choose to assign to them and how well they serve those functions. This is the feature of intentionality I am calling "the assignment—or imposition—of function." In the case of some artifacts, we build the object to serve a function. Chairs, bathtubs, and computers are obvious examples. In the case of many naturally occurring objects, such as rivers and trees, we assign a function—aesthetic, practical, and so on—to a preexisting object. We say, "That river is good to swim in," or "That type of tree can be used for lumber."

The important thing to see at this point is that functions are never intrinsic to the physics of any phenomenon but are assigned from outside by conscious observers and users. *Functions, in short, are never intrinsic but are always observer relative.*

We are blinded to this fact by the practice, especially in biology, of talking of functions as if they were intrinsic to nature. But except for those parts of nature that are conscious, nature knows nothing of functions. It is, for example, intrinsic to nature that the heart pumps blood, and causes it to course through the body. It is also an intrinsic fact of nature that the movement of the blood is related to a whole lot of other causal processes having to do with the survival of the organism. But when, in addition to saying "The heart pumps blood" we say, "The *function* of the heart is to pump blood," we are doing something more than recording these intrinsic facts.

We are situating these facts relative to a system of values that we hold. It is intrinsic to us that we hold these values, but the attribution of these values to nature independent of us is observer relative. Even when we *discover* a function in nature, as when we discovered the function of the heart, the discovery consists in the discovery of the causal processes together with the assignment of a teleology to those causal processes. This is shown by the fact that a whole vocabulary of success and failure is now appropriate that is not appropriate to simple brute facts of nature. Thus we can speak of "malfunction," "heart disease," and better and worse hearts. We do not speak of better and worse stones, unless of course we have assigned a function to the stone. If we use the stone as a weapon or a paperweight or an *objet d'art trouvé*, for example, we can asses its adequacy under these functional descriptions.

This point has to be understood precisely. We do indeed "discover" functions in nature. But the *discovery* of a natural function can take place only within a set of prior *assignments* of value (including purposes, teleology, and other functions). Thus given that we already accept that for organisms there is a value in survival and reproduction, and that for a species there is a value in continued existence, we can *discover* that the function of the heart is to pump blood, the function of the vestibular ocular reflex is to stabilize the retinal image, and so on. When we discover such a natural function, there are no natural facts discovered beyond the causal facts. Part of what the vocabulary of "functions" adds to the vocabulary of "causes" is a set of values (including purposes and teleology generally). It is because we take it for granted in biology that life and survival are values that we can discover that the function of the heart is to pump blood. If we thought the most important value in the world was to glorify God by making thumping noises, then the function of the heart would be to make a thumping noise, and the noisier heart would be the better heart. If we valued death and extinction above all, then we would say that a function of cancer is to speed death. The function of aging would be to hasten death, and the function of natural selection would be extinction. In all these functional assignments, no new intrinsic facts are involved. As far as nature is concerned intrinsically, there are no functional facts beyond causal facts. The further assignment of function is observer relative.

One of Darwin's greatest achievements was to drive teleology out of the account of the origin of species. On the Darwinian account, evolution occurs by way of blind, brute, natural forces. There is no intrinsic purpose whatever to the origin and survival of biological species. We can, arbitrarily, define the "functions" of biological processes relative to the survival of organisms, but the idea that any such assignment of function is a matter of the discovery of an intrinsic teleology in nature, and that functions are therefore intrinsic, is always subject to a variant of Moore's open-question argument: What is so functional about functions, so defined? Either "function" is defined in terms of causes, in which case there is nothing intrinsically functional about functions, they are just causes like any others. Or functions are defined in terms of the furtherance of a set of values that we hold—life, survival, reproduction, health—in which case they are observer relative.

I realize that many biologists and philosophers of biology will disagree. Over the past few decades there has developed a large literature on functions and functional explanations. Much of it is influenced by Larry Wright's article[3] in which he defines function as follows:

The function of X is Z *means*

1. X is there because it does Z.

2. Z is a consequence (or result) of X's being there.

If such an analysis were correct, it would eliminate the observer relativity of function. Intuitively the idea is to define "function" in terms of causation: X performs the function F just in case X causes F, and at least part of the explanation for X's existence is that it causes F. Thus, for example, the heart has the function of pumping blood because it does pump blood and the explanation for the existence of hearts in evolutionary history is that they do in fact pump blood. This seems to give a naturalistic definition of "function" whereby functions would be intrinsic. Ruth Millikan has a similar, but more complex, idea in her notion of "proper function," though she insists that she is not trying to analyze the ordinary use of the notion of function but to introduce a new technical expression defined in terms of "reproduction" and causation.* So construed no one could object. You can introduce any new technical terms you like. However, it is important to emphasize that such definitions fail to capture certain essential features of the ordinary notion of function, for at least three reasons. First, in Millikan's case it makes the definition of function dependent on a particular causal historical theory about "reproduction." In fact I believe my heart functions to pump blood and I also believe in a Darwinian account of how "reproduction" gives a causal historical account of the evolution of hearts. But even if no such account of reproduction, Darwinian or otherwise, turned out to be true, my heart would still function to pump blood. On her definition the

---

*R. G. Millikan, *Language, Thought, and Other Biological Categories: New Foundations for Realism* (Cambridge, Mass.: MIT Press, 1984). In R. G. Millikan, "In Defense of Proper Functions," in *The Philosophy of Science* 56 (1989), 288–302. She writes:

> The definition of a "proper function" is recursive. Putting things very roughly, for an item A to have a function F as a "proper function," it is necessary (and close to sufficient) that one of these two conditions should hold. (1) A originated as a "reproduction" (to give one example, as a copy, or a copy of a copy) of some prior item or items that, *due* in part to possession of the properties reproduced, have actually performed F in the past, and A exists because (causally historically because) of this or these performances. (2) A originated as the product of some prior device that, given its circumstances, had performance of F as a proper function and that, under those circumstances normally causes F to be performed by *means* of producing an item like A. Items that fall under condition (2) have "derived proper functions," functions derived from the functions of the devices that produce them.(p. 288)

very meaning of the claim that the heart has the (proper) function of pumping blood can be explained only in terms of a causal historical account of how hearts are reproduced, and that cannot be right as far as our ordinary notion of function is concerned. Second, if we take such definitions as capturing the essential features of our ordinary notion, there are counterexamples to the analyses. On Wright's account and apparently on Millikan's as well, we would have to say that the function (proper or otherwise) of colds is to spread cold germs. They do in fact spread cold germs, and if they did not spread cold germs they would not exist. But on our ordinary notion colds do not have a function, or if they do it is certainly not to spread germs. Third, the normative component of functions is left unexplained. Though analyses such as Millikan's can account for the fact that some entities that have a function do not in fact carry out the function, the reduction of function to causal notions still leaves out the normative component. Why do we talk of malfunctioning hearts, of heart disease, of better and worse hearts? The usual dilemma shows up: either we are talking about brute, blind causal relations, in which case hearts pumping blood and colds spreading germs are in the same basket, or we think there is something really functional about functions, in which case this type of definition leaves out the observer-relative feature.

Another, and perhaps decisive, clue that functions, unlike causes, are observer relative is that functional attributions, unlike causal attributions, are intensional-with-an-s.* Substitution of coreferential terms in function contexts fails to guarantee preser-

---

*Intensionality-with-an-s should not be confused with intentionality-with-a-t. Intentionality is that property of the mind by which it is directed at objects and states of affairs in the world. Intensionality is that property of sentences and other representations by which they fail certain test for extensionality. One of the most famous of these is Leibniz's Law: If two expressions refer to the same object they can be substituted for each other in a sentence without changing the truth value of the sentence. Sentences that fail this test are said to be *intensional* with respect to substitutability. Another expression used to name this sort of invation of truth value. Thus "The function of A is to X" together with "X-ing is identical with Y-ing" do not imply "The function of A is to Y." For example, it is trivially true that the function of oars is to row with, and rowing consists in exerting pressure on water relative to a fixed fulcrum; but it is not the case that the function of oars is to exert pressure on water relative to a fixed fulcrum.

To summarize, the first feature we need to note in our discussion of the capacity of conscious agents to create social facts is the assignment of functions to objects and to other phenomena. Functions are never intrinsic; they are assigned relative to the interests of users and observers.

I have not attempted to analyze the sentence form "The function of X is to Y" into logically necessary and sufficient conditions. But I am calling attention to certain central conditions.

1. Whenever the function of X is to Y, X and Y are parts of a *system* where the system is in part defined by *purposes, goals, and values generally.* This is why there are functions of policemen and professors but no function of humans as such—unless we think of humans as part of some larger system where their function is, e.g., to serve God.

2. Whenever the function of X is to Y, then X is *supposed to* cause or otherwise result in Y. This normative component in functions cannot be reduced to causation alone, to what in fact happens as a result of X, because X can have the function of Y-ing even in cases where X fails to bring about Y all or even most of the time. Thus the function of safety valves is to prevent explosions, and this is true even for valves that are so badly made that they in fact fail to prevent explosions, i.e., they *malfunction.*

---

tensionality is "referential opacity." Typically sentences that are about intentional-with-a-t states are intensional-with-an-s sentences, because in such sentences the way in which an object is referred to affects the truth value of the sentence. For extensive discussion of these matters see Searle, *Intentionality, An Essay in the Philosophy of Mind.*

The examples we have considered so far suggest a further distinction between *agentive* and *nonagentive* functions. Sometimes the assignment of function has to do with our immediate purposes, whether practical, gastronomic, esthetic, educational, or whatever. When we say, "This stone is a paperweight," "This object is a screwdriver," or "This is a chair," these three functional notions mark *uses* to which we put objects, functions that we do not discover, and that do not occur naturally, but that are assigned relative to the practical interests of conscious agents. Not all these interests are "practical" in any ordinary sense, because such functions are also assigned when we say "That is an ugly painting." Because all these are instance of uses to which agents intentionally put objects, I will call them "agentive functions." Some of the objects to which we assign agentive functions are naturally occurring, such as a stone that we use as a paperweight; some are artifacts made specifically to perform these functions, such as chairs, screwdrivers, and oil paintings. An object manufactured to perform one agentive function can be used to perform another, as reported, e.g., by "This hammer is my paperweight." As in the case of the heart, the function is not intrinsic to the object in addition to its causal relations, but in contrast to the ascription of function to the heart, in these cases the ascription of the function ascribes the *use to which we intentionally put* these objects.

Some functions are not imposed on objects to serve practical purposes but are assigned to naturally occurring objects and processes as part of a theoretical account of the phenomena in question. Thus we say "The heart functions to pump blood" when we are giving an account of how organisms live and survive. Relative to a teleology that values survival and reproduction, we can discover such functions occurring in nature independently of the practical intentions and activities of human agents; so let us call these functions "nonagentive functions."[4]

There is no sharp dividing line between the two, and sometimes an agentive function can replace a nonagentive function, as when, for example, we make an "artificial heart." It is generally, though by no means always, the case that agentive functions require continuous intentionality on the part of users for their maintenance, whereas nonagentive functions continue to chug functionally along without any effort on our part. Thus bathtubs, coins, and screwdrivers require continued use on our part in order to function as bathtubs, coins, and screwdrivers, but hearts and livers continue to function as hearts and livers even when no one is paying any attention. Furthermore, the person actually using some object for an agentive function may not be the agent who actually imposed the function on that object and may even be unaware that the object has that function. Thus most car drivers are probably unaware that the function of the drive shaft is to transmit power from the transmission to the axles, but all the same that is its agentive function.

One more distinction: Within agentive functions we need to identify a special class. Sometimes the agentive function assigned to an object is that of standing for or representing something else. Thus, when I draw a diagram of a football play, I let certain circles stand for the quarterback, the runningback, the offensive linemen, and so on. In this case, the agentive function assigned to the marks on the paper is that of representing or standing for; but because "representing" and "standing for" are just other names for intentionality, in this case we have intentionally imposed intentionality on objects and states of affairs that are not intrinsically intentional. There are names in English for the result of this type of imposition of function: They are called "meaning" or "symbolism." Marks on the paper now have meaning in a way that a screwdriver, for example, does not have meaning, because the marks on the paper now stand for or represent objects and states of affairs independent of themselves. The most famous sorts of meaning are, of course, in language. In the use of language we impose a specific function, namely, that of representing, onto marks and sounds.

I said earlier that the capacity to impose functions on natural phenomena was remarkable, but equally remarkable is the fact that functions may be imposed quite unconsciously, and the functions once imposed are often—so to speak—invisible. So, for example, money may simply have evolved without anyone ever thinking, "We are now imposing a new function on these objects"; and once money has evolved, people may use money to buy and sell without thinking about the logical structure of imposed function. However, for all cases of agentive function, someone must be capable of understanding what the thing is for, or the function could never be assigned. At least some of the participants in the system of exchange must understand, consciously or unconsciously, that money is to buy things with, screwdrivers are for driving screws, and so forth. If we assign a function that is totally apart from human intentions, it would have to fall in the category of nonagentive functions. Thus suppose someone says that the intended agentive function of money is to serve as a medium of exchange and a store of value, but money also serves the hidden, secret, unintended function of maintaining the system of power relationships in society. The first claim is about the intentionality of agentive function. The second claim is about nonagentive function. To see this, simply ask yourself what facts in the world would make each claim true. The first claim is made true by the intentionality with which agents use objects as money. They use it *for the purpose of* buying, selling, and storing value. The second claim, like the claim that the heart functions to pump blood, would be true if and only if there is a set of unintended causal relations and these serve some teleology, even if it is not a teleology shared by the speaker. Some social scientists speak of a distinction between manifest and latent function. If this distinction parallels the distinction I have been making, then manifest functions are agentive functions and latent functions are nonagentive.

To summarize these points, we have discovered three separate categories of the assignment of function. First, nonagentive functions: For example, the function of the heart is to pump blood. In general these nonagentive functions are naturally occurring. Second, agentive functions: For example, the function of a screwdriver is to install and remove screws. Third, within agentive functions a special subclass, where the function assigned is that of intentionality: For example, the function of the sentence "Snow is white" is to represent, truly or falsely, the state of affairs that snow is white.[5]

Just to keep the terminology straight I will adopt the following conventions.

1. Since all functions are observer relative I will speak of all functions as *assigned* or equivalently as *imposed.*

2. Within the category of assigned functions some are *agentive* because they are matters of the use to which agents put entities, e.g., the function of bathtubs is to take baths in.

3. Within the category of assigned functions some are *nonagentive* because they are naturally occurring causal processes to which we have assigned a purpose, e.g., the function of the heart is to pump blood.

4. Within the category of agentive functions is a special category of those entities whose agentive function is to *symbolize, represent, stand for,* or—in general—to *mean* something or other.

Collective Intentionality

Many species of animals, our own especially, have a capacity for collective intentionality. By this I mean not only that they engage in cooperative behavior, but that they share intentional states such as beliefs, desires, and intentions. In addition to singular intentionality there is also collective intentionality. Obvious examples are cases where *I* am doing something only as part of *our* doing something. So if I am an offensive lineman playing in a football game, I might be blocking the defensive end, but I am blocking only as part of *our* executing a pass play. If I am a violinist in an orchestra I play *my* part in *our* performance of the symphony.

Even most forms of human conflict require collective intentionality. In order that two men should engage in a prizefight, for example, there has to be collective intentionality at a higher level. They have to be cooperating in having a fight in order for each of them to try to beat the other up. In this respect, prizefighting differs from simply beating up someone in an alley. The man who creeps up behind another man in an alley and assaults him is not engaging in collective behavior. But two prizefighters, as well as opposing litigants in a court case, and even two faculty members trading insults at a cocktail party, are all engaged in cooperative collective behavior at a higher level, within which the antagonistic hostile behavior can take place. An understanding of collective intentionality is essential to understanding social facts.

What is the relation between singular and collective intentionality, between, for example, the facts described by "I intend" and "We intend"? Most efforts I have seen to answer this question try to reduce "We intentionality" to "I intentionality" plus something else, usually mutual beliefs. The idea is that if we intend to do something together, then that consists in the fact that I intend to do it in the belief that you also intend to do it; and you intend to do it in the belief that I also intend to do it. And each believes that the other has these beliefs, and has these beliefs about these beliefs, and these beliefs about these beliefs about these beliefs . . . etc., in a potentially infinite hierarchy of beliefs. "I believe that you believe that I believe that you believe that I believe. . . . ," and so on. In my view all these efforts to reduce collective intentionality to individual intentionality fail. Collective intentionality is a biologically primitive phenomenon that cannot be reduced to or eliminated in favor of something else. Every attempt at reducing "We intentionality" to "I intentionality" that I have seen is subject to counterexamples.[6]

There is a deep reason why collective intentionality cannot be reduced to individual intentionality. The problem with believing that you believe that I believe, etc., and you believing that I believe that you believe, etc., is that it does not add up to a sense of *collectivity*. No set of "I Consciousnesses," even supplemented with beliefs, adds up to a "We Consciousness." The crucial element in collective intentionality is a sense of doing (wanting, believing, etc.) something together, and the individual intentionality that each person has is derived *from* the collective intentionality that they share. Thus, to go back to the earlier example of the football game, I do indeed have a singular intention to block the defensive end, but I have that intention only as part of our collective intention to execute a pass play.

We can see these differences quite starkly if we contrast the case where there is genuine cooperative behavior with the cases where, so to speak, by accident two people happen to find that their behavior is synchronized. There is a big difference between two violinists playing in an orchestra, on the one hand, and on the other hand, discovering, while I am practicing my part, that someone in the next room is practicing her part, and thus discovering that, by chance, we are playing the same piece in a synchronized fashion.

Why are so many philosophers convinced that collective intentionality must be reducible to individual intentionality? Why are they unwilling to recognize collective intentionality as a primitive phenomenon? I believe the reason is that they accept an argument that looks appealing but is fallacious. The argument is that because all intentionality exists in the heads of individual human beings, the form of that intentionality can make reference only to the individuals in whose heads it exists. So it has seemed that anybody who recognizes collective intentionality as a primitive form of mental life must be committed to the idea that there exists some Hegelian world spirit, a collective consciousness, or something equally implausible. The requirements of methodological individualism seem to force us to reduce collective intentionality to individual intentionality. It has seemed, in short, that we have to choose between reductionism, on the one hand, or a super mind floating over individual minds, on the other. I want to claim, on the contrary, that the argument contains a fallacy and that the dilemma is a false one. It is indeed the case that all my mental life is inside my brain, and all your mental life is inside your brain, and so on for everybody else. But it does not follow from that that all my mental life must be expressed in the form of a singular

noun phrase referring to me. The form that my collective intentionality can take is simply "we intend," "we are doing so-and-so,"
and the like. In such cases, I intend only as part of our intending.
The intentionality that exists in each individual head has the form
"we intend."[7]

The traditional picture of "we intentions" looks like this:

Figure 1.1

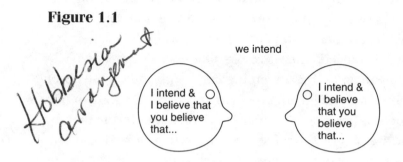

The alternative that I am proposing looks like this:

Figure 1.2

By stipulation I will henceforth use the expression "social fact" to
refer to any fact involving collective intentionality. So, for example,
the fact that two people are going for a walk together is a social
fact. A special subclass of social facts are institutional facts, facts
involving human institutions. So, for example, the fact that this
piece of paper is a twenty dollar bill is an institutional fact. I will
have a great deal more to say about institutional facts.

Constitutive Rules and the Distinction Between
Brute and Institutional Facts

In my work on the philosophy of language[8] I suggested the beginnings of an answer to the question concerning the relationships between those features of the world that are matters of brute physics and biology, on the one hand, and those features of the world that are matters of culture and society, on the other. Without implying that these are the only kinds of facts that exist in the world, we need to distinguish between *brute facts* such as the fact that the sun is ninety-three million miles from the earth and *institutional* facts such as the fact that Clinton is president. Brute facts exist independently of any human institutions; institutional facts can exist only within human institutions. Brute facts require the institution of language in order that we can *state* the facts, but the brute facts *themselves* exist quite independently of language or of any other institution. Thus the *statement* that the sun is ninety-three million miles from the earth requires an institution of language and an institution of measuring distances in miles, but the *fact stated,* the fact that there is a certain distance between the earth and the sun, exists independently of any institution. Institutional facts, on the other hand, require special human institutions for their very existence. Language is one such institution; indeed, it is a whole set of such institutions.

And what are these "institutions"? To answer this question, I introduced another distinction, the distinction between what I call "regulative" and "constitutive" rules.[9] Some rules regulate antecedently existing activities. For example, the rule "drive on the right-hand side of the road" regulates driving; but driving can exist prior to the existence of that rule. However, some rules do not merely regulate, they also create the very possibility of certain activities. Thus the rules of chess do not regulate an antecedently existing activity. It is not the case that there were a lot of people pushing bits of wood around on boards, and in order to prevent them from bumping into each other all the time and creating traffic jams, we had to regulate the activity. Rather, the rules of chess create the very possibility of playing chess. The rules are *constitutive* of chess in the sense that playing chess is constituted in part by acting in accord with the rules. If you don't follow at least a large subset of the rules, you are not playing chess. The rules come in systems, and the rules individually, or sometimes the system collectively, characteristically have the form

"X counts as Y" or "X counts as Y in context C."

Thus, such and such counts as a checkmate, such and such a move counts as a legal pawn move, and so on.

The claim I made was, institutional facts exist only within systems of constitutive rules. The systems of rules create the possibility of facts of this type; and specific instances of institutional facts such as the fact that I won at chess or the fact that Clinton is president are created by the application of specific rules, rules for checkmate or for electing and swearing in presidents, for example. It is perhaps important to emphasize that I am discussing *rules* and not *conventions*. It is a rule of chess that we win the game by checkmating the king. It is a *convention* of chess that the king is larger than a pawn. "Convention" implies arbitrariness, but constitutive rules in general are not in that sense arbitrary.

The context "X counts as Y in C" is intensional-with-an-s. It is referentially opaque in that it does not permit of substitutability of coextensive expressions *salva veritate*. Thus, for example, the statements:

1. Bills issued by the Bureau of Engraving and Printing(X) count as money(Y) in the United States(C).

and

2. Money is the root of all evil.

do not imply

3. Bills issued by the Bureau of Engraving and Printing count as the root of all evil in the United States.

As always the discovery of referential opacity is a crucial point. In this case it provides a clue that there is a mental component in institutional facts. The intentionality-with-an-s of the verbal formulation is a clue that the phenomena represented are intentional-with-a-t. A great deal hangs on this, as we will see in subsequent chapters.

Various social theorists have attacked my account of the distinction between regulative and constitutive rules,[10] but I think my account is right as far as it goes. The problem is that for our present purposes it does not go far enough. We still need a more thorough account of rules and institutions. And we need to answer a lot of questions. Are all social facts institutional facts? Are there constitutive rules of, for example, wars and cocktail parties? What makes something into a "constitutive rule" anyway? Hardest of all, how do we make the connection between the fundamental ontology of conscious biological beasts like ourselves and the apparatus of social facts and human institutions?

I will have more to say later about the form of constitutive rules and how they relate to the ontology of institutional facts. My aim in this chapter is to assemble the pieces, and I now have the three I need: the imposition of function on entities that do not have that function prior to the imposition, collective intentionality, and the distinction between constitutive and regulative rules. With these in hand we can now turn to the construction of institutional reality.

2

Creating Institutional Facts

In this chapter I describe the elementary construction of social facts and the logical structure of the development of institutional facts from simpler forms of social facts. To do so, I will use the apparatus of agentive functions, collective intentionality, and constitutive rules. I will also attempt to explain several puzzling features of social reality.

Some Apparent Features of Social Reality

To begin, let us identify some of the apparent features of social reality we would like to explain. Because I believe philosophical investigations should begin naively (how they proceed and conclude is another matter), I will simply list half a dozen of what appear to be naive, intuitive features of social reality, including features of institutional facts, such as, for example, the fact that I am an American citizen, as well as features of those social facts that do not require institutional structures, such as, for example, the fact that two men are pushing a car together to try to get it started.

1.   *The Self-Referentiality of Many Social Concepts*

The concepts that name social facts appear to have a peculiar kind of self-referentiality. As a preliminary formulation we can say, for example, in order that the concept "money" apply to the stuff in my pocket, it has to be the sort of thing that people think is money. If everybody stops believing it is money, it ceases to function as money, and eventually ceases to be money. Logically speaking, the statement "A certain type of substance, x, is money" implies an indefinite inclusive disjunction of the form "x is used as money or x is regarded as money or x is believed to be money, etc." But that seems to have the consequence that the concept of money, the very definition of the word "money," is self-referential, because in order that a type of thing should satisfy the definition, in order that it should fall under the concept of money, it must be believed to be, or used as, or regarded as, etc., satisfying the definition. For these sorts of facts, it seems to be almost a logical truth that you cannot fool all the people all the time. If everybody always thinks that this sort of thing is money, and they use it as money and treat it as money, then it is money. If nobody ever thinks this sort of thing is money, then it is not money. And what goes for money goes for elections, private property, wars, voting, promises, marriages, buying and selling, political offices, and so on.

In order to state this point precisely we need to distinguish between institutions and general practices on the one hand and particular instances on the other, that is, we need to distinguish between types and tokens. A single dollar bill might fall from the printing presses into the cracks of the floor and never be used or thought of as money at all, but it would still be money. In such a case a particular token instance would be money, even though no one ever thought it was money or thought about it or used it at all. Similarly, there might be a counterfeit dollar bill in circulation even if no one ever knew that it was counterfeit, not even the counterfeiter. In such a case everyone who used that particular token would think it was money even though it was not in fact money. About particular tokens it is possible for people to be systematically mistaken. But where the *type* of thing is concerned, the belief that the type is a type of money is constitutive of its being money in a way we will need to make fully clear.

For some institutional phenomena, such as money, what I say applies more to types than tokens, for others, such as cocktail parties, it applies to each individual token. For the sake of simplicity I will assume that the reader is aware of the distinction, and I will speak of the self-referentiality of institutional concepts in general, without making the distinction in every case. Later I will try to explain the difference between self-referentiality as applied to types and as applied to tokens.

But if the *type* of thing in question is money only because people believe it to be money, if "money" implies "regarded as, used as, or believed to be money," then philosophers will get worried, because the claim seems to produce either a vicious infinite regress or a vicious circle. If part of the content of the claim that something is money is the claim that it is believed to be money, then what is the content of that belief? If the content of the belief that something is money contains in part the belief that it is money, then the belief that something is money is in part the belief that it is believed to be money; and there is, in turn, no way to explain the content of that belief without repeating the same feature over and over again. Later on, I will try to show how to avoid this infinite regress. At this point, I am just calling attention to a peculiar logical feature that distinguishes social concepts from such natural concepts as "mountain" or "molecule." Something can be a mountain even if no one believes it is a mountain; something can be a molecule even if no one thinks anything at all about it. But for social facts, the attitude that we take toward the phenomenon is partly constitutive of the phenomenon. If, for example, we give a big cocktail party, and invite everyone in Paris, and if things get out of hand, and it turns out that the casualty rate is greater than the Battle of Austerlitz—all the same, it is not a war; it is just one amazing cocktail party. Part of being a cocktail party is being thought to be a cocktail party; part of being a war is being thought to be a war. This is a remarkable feature of social facts; it has no analogue among physical facts.

2.   The Use of Performative Utterances in the Creation of Institutional Facts

One of the most fascinating features of institutional facts is that a very larger number, though by no means all of them, can be created by explicit performative utterances. Performatives are members of the class of speech acts I call "declarations."[1] In declarations the state of affairs represented by the propositional content of the speech act is brought into existence by the successful performance of that very speech act. Institutional facts can be created with the performative utterance of such sentences as "The meeting is adjourned," "I give and bequeath my entire fortune to my nephew," "I appoint you chairman," "War is hereby declared," etc. These utterances create the very state of affairs that they represent; and in each case, the state of affairs is an institutional fact.

3.   The Logical Priority of Brute Facts over Institutional Facts

Intuitively it seems there are no institutional facts without brute facts. For example, just about any sort of substance can be money, but money has to exist in some physical form or other. Money can be bits of metal, slips of paper, wampum, or entries in books. In fact, most of our money in the past couple of decades underwent a revolutionary physical transformation that we did not even notice. Most money is now in the form of magnetic traces on computer disks. It does not matter what the form is as long as it can *function* as money, but money must come in some physical form or other.

What is true of money is true of chess games, elections, and universities. All these can take different forms, but for each there must be some physical realization. This suggests what I think is true, that social facts in general, and institutional facts especially, are hierarchically structured. Institutional facts exist, so to speak, on top of brute physical facts. Often, the brute facts will not be manifested as physical objects but as sounds coming out of peoples' mouths or as marks on paper—or even thoughts in their heads.

4. Systematic Relationships Among Institutional Facts.

An institutional fact cannot exist in isolation but only in a set of systematic relations to other facts. Thus, for example, in order that anybody in a society could have money, that society must have a system of exchanging goods and services for money. But in order that it can have a system of exchange, it must have a system of property and property ownership. Similarly, in order that societies should have marriages, they must have some form of contractual relationships. But in order that they can have contractual relationships, they have to understand such things as promises and obligations.

Furthermore, quite apart from the logical or conceptual requirement of interrelationships of institutional facts, it just turns out that in any real life situation one will find oneself in a complex of interlocking institutional realities. The restaurant scene described in Chapter 1 illustrates this: at any instant in the scene, one is (at least) a citizen, an owner of money, a client, a bill payer; and one is dealing with property, a restaurant, a waiter, a bill.

It might seem that games are counterexamples to this general principle, because, of course, games are designed to be forms of activity that do not connect with the rest of our lives in a way that institutional facts characteristically do. Today's philosophy department softball game need have no consequences for tomorrow, in a way that today's wars, revolutions, buyings, and sellings are intended precisely to have consequences for tomorrow and into the indefinite future.* Nonetheless, even in the case of games, there are systematic dependencies on other forms of institutional facts. The position of the pitcher, the catcher, and the batter, for example, all involve rights and responsibilities; and their positions and actions or inactions are unintelligible without an understanding of these rights and responsibilities; but these notions are in turn unintelligible without the general notion of rights and responsibilities.

5.   The Primacy of Social Acts over Social Objects, of Processes over Products

It is tempting to think of *social objects* as independently existing entities on analogy with the objects studied by the natural sciences. It is tempting to think that a government or a dollar bill or a contract is an object or entity in the sense that a DNA molecule, a tectonic plate, or a planet is an object or entity. In the case of social objects, however, the grammar of the noun phrases conceals from us the fact that, in such cases, process is prior to product. Social objects are always, in some sense we will need to explain, constituted by social acts; and, in a sense, *the object is just the continuous possibility of the activity*. A twenty dollar bill, for example, is a standing possibility of paying for something.

---

*To the extent that professional sports have such consequences, they cease to be just games and become something more, e.g., big business.

6.　The Linguistic Component of Many Institutional Facts

Related to features 1 and 2 is the further apparent feature that only beings that have a language or some more or less language-like system of representation can create most, perhaps all, institutional facts, because *the linguistic element appears to be partly constitutive of the fact.*

It is common, for example, to read that certain ant colonies have slaves or that beehives have queens. I think such manners of speaking are harmless metaphors, especially where the so called "social insects" are concerned, but it is important to keep reminding ourselves that for a community literally to have slaves or literally to have a queen, the participants would have to have the apparatus necessary to represent something as a queen or as a slave. Just behaving in certain ways, where behavior is construed solely in terms of bodily movements, is not sufficient for a community to have a queen or to have slaves. In addition, there would have to be a certain set of attitudes, beliefs, etc., on the part of the members of the community, and this would seem to require a system of representation such as language. Language seems to be essential not only to represent these facts to ourselves; but in a way that we will have to explain, the linguistic forms in question are partly constitutive of the facts. But what *exactly* is the role of language in the constitution of institutional facts? This is not an easy question, and we will devote the next chapter to answering it.

From Collective Intentionality to Institutional Facts: The Example of Money

The simplest form of social facts involves simple forms of collective behavior. As I said earlier, I think the capacity for collective behavior is biologically innate, and the forms of collective intentionality cannot be eliminated or reduced to something else. For example, it takes no cultural apparatus, cultural conventions, or language for animals to move together in a pack or to hunt together. When hyenas move in a pack to kill an isolated lion, no linguistic or cultural apparatus is necessary, even though the behavior of the hyenas is very skillfully coordinated and the hyenas are responsive not only to the lion but to each other. The selectional advantage of cooperative behavior is, I trust, obvious. Inclusive fitness is increased by cooperating with conspecifics.

The only tricky feature of assimilating collective animal behavior into a general theory of intentionality derives from the fact that in any complex form of behavior, such as the example of hyenas attacking a lion, each animal's individual contribution to the collective behavior will have a different intentional content from the collective intentionality. In the case of humans, for example, if our team is executing a pass play, and my assignment is to block the defensive end, then my individual intentionality is, "I am blocking the defensive end"; but that has a different content from the collective intentionality, "We are executing a pass play," even though I am blocking the defensive end only as part of our executing the pass play. The content of the individual intentionality, then, may vary from the content of the collective intentionality, even though the individual's intentionality is part of the collective. It takes two to tango and more than two to execute a pass play.[2] As a step in developing a hierarchical taxonomy of social and institutional reality, I have already stipulated that any fact involving collective intentionality is a social fact. Thus, for example, hyenas hunting a lion and Congress passing legislation are both cases of social facts. Institutional facts, it will turn out, are a special subclass of social facts. Congress passing legislation is an institutional fact; hyenas hunting a lion is not.

The next step is the introduction of agentive functions of a collective sort. Given an apparatus that includes both collective intentionality and the intentional imposition of agentive functions on physical objects, it is no big step to combine the two. If it is easy to see how a single person might decide to use some object as a chair or a lever, then I believe it is not difficult to see how two or more people together could decide to use some object as a bench on which they can all sit or to use something as a lever to be operated by several people, rather than just one. Collective intentionality can generate agentive functions as easily as individual intentionality.

The next step is more difficult because it involves the collective imposition of functions on objects where the function assigned to the object cannot be performed solely in virtue of the object's intrinsic physical features, as was the case for a log used as a bench, or a stick used as a lever. In this next type of case, the function is itself performed only as a matter of human cooperation. We will see in some detail that this step, the collective imposition of function, where the function can be performed only in virtue of collective agreement or acceptance, is a crucial element in the creation of institutional facts.

Consider for example a primitive tribe that initially builds a wall around its territory. The wall is an instance of a function imposed in virtue of sheer physics: the wall, we will suppose, is big enough to keep intruders out and the members of the tribe in. But suppose the wall gradually evolves from being a physical barrier to being a symbolic barrier. Imagine that the wall gradually decays so that the only thing left is a line of stones. But imagine that the inhabitants and their neighbors continue to *recognize* the line of stones as marking the boundary of the territory in such a way that it affects their behavior. For example, the inhabitants only cross the boundary under special conditions, and outsiders can only cross into the territory if it is acceptable to the inhabitants. The line of stones now has a function that is not performed in virtue of sheer physics but in virtue of collective intentionality. Unlike a high wall or a moat, the wall remnant cannot keep people out simply because of its physical constitution. The result is, in a very primitive sense, symbolic; because a set of physical objects now performs the function of indicating something beyond itself, namely, the limits of the territory.* The line of stones performs the same *function* as a physical barrier but it does not do so in virtue of its physical construction, but because it has been collectively assigned a new *status*, the status of a boundary marker.

I would like this step to seem a most natural and innocent development, but it is momentous in its implications. Animals can impose functions on natural phenomena. Consider, for example, the primates that use a stick as a tool to get bananas that are out of reach.[3] And some primates have even developed traditions of agentive functions that are transmitted from one generation to the next. Thus, most famously Imo, a Japanese macaque, used water to get the sand off her potatoes and eventually salt water both to get the sand off and to improve the flavor. Thanks to Imo, "today," writes Kummer, "potato-washing in salt water is an established tradition which infants learn from their mother as a natural adjunct of eating potatoes."[4] Anthropology texts routinely remark on the human capacity for tool using. But the truly radical break with other forms of life comes when humans, through collective intentionality, impose functions on phenomena where the function cannot be achieved solely in virtue of physics and chemistry but requires continued human cooperation in the specific forms of recognition, acceptance, and acknowledgment of a new *status* to which a *function* is assigned. This is the beginning point of all institutional forms of human culture, and it must always have the structure X counts as Y in C, as we shall see later.

---

*In an earlier version of this argument, I used the ethologists' example of groups of animals marking limits to their territory. In such a case, as in the example of the primitive tribe, the barrier is not a sheer physical obstacle like a wall or a moat but is, in some sense, symbolic. But I am not certain that the ethologists are justified in attributing so much collective intentionality to the animals, so I have substituted the tribal example to make the same point. When we discuss the role of language in the next chapter we will see that the distinction between the linguistic and the prelinguistic is important.

Our aim is to assimilate social reality to our basic ontology of physics, chemistry, and biology. To do this we need to show the continuous line that goes from molecules and mountains to screwdrivers, levers, and beautiful sunsets, and then to legislatures, money, and nation-states. The central span on the bridge from physics to society is collective intentionality, and the decisive movement on that bridge in the creation of social reality is the collective intentional imposition of function on entities that cannot perform those functions without that imposition. The radical movement that gets us from such simple social facts as that we are sitting on a bench together or having a fistfight to such institutional facts as money, property, and marriage is the collective imposition of function on entities, which—unlike levers, benches, and cars—cannot perform the functions solely by virtue of their physical structure. In some cases, paper currency, for example, this is because the structure is only incidentally related to the function; in other cases, licensed drivers, for example, it is because we do not allow people to perform the function of driving unless they have been *authorized.*

The key element in the move from the collective imposition of function to the creation of institutional facts is the imposition of a collectively recognized *status* to which a function is attached. Since this is a special category of agentive functions, I will label these *status functions*. In the case of the boundary, we imagined a causally functioning physical object, a wall, evolving into a symbolic object, a boundary marker. The boundary is intended to function in the same way that the wall did, but the means by which it performs this function is the collective recognition of the stones as having a special status to which the function is attached. In the extreme case, the status function may be attached to an entity whose physical structure is only arbitrarily related to the performance of the function. As an illustration, consider the case of money and especially the evolution of paper currency. Standard textbook accounts of money identify three kinds: *commodity money,* such as gold, is regarded as valuable, and hence as money, because the commodity itself is regarded as valuable; *contract money* consists of bits of paper that are regarded as valuable because they are promissory notes to pay the bearer in valuable commodities such as gold; and *fiat money* consists of bits of paper that are declared to be valuable as money by some official agency such as a government or a central bank. So far, though, it is not clear what the relationship among these three is, or even what fact about all three makes it the case that they are all money. In the case of commodity money the stuff is a medium of exchange because it is valuable; in the case of fiat money the stuff is valuable because it is a medium of exchange.

The logical relations among these three can be illustrated by the standard account of the evolution of paper currency in medieval Europe. I will assume this account is true, but it does not really matter much for our present purposes. I am using the account only to illustrate certain logical relations, which do not depend on its historical accuracy. Here is how it goes. The use of commodity money, such as gold and silver, is, in effect, a form of barter, because the form that the money takes is regarded as itself valuable. Thus the substance in question performs the function of money solely because of its physical nature, which will typically already have some function imposed on it. Thus, gold coins are valuable not because they are coins but because they are made of gold, and the value attached to the coin is exactly equal to the value attached to the gold in it. We impose the function of "value" on the substance gold because we desire to possess that kind of substance. Because the function of value has already been imposed on gold, it is easy to impose the function of money on top of the function of value. And that is just a fancy way of saying that because people already regard gold as valuable because of its physical nature, they are willing to accept it as a medium of exchange. We thus have a system of exchange where objects are held for the purposes of barter, even though the people holding those objects may have no interest in them or use for them, as such. A similar situation existed, by the way, in the former Soviet Union at the time of its collapse. In Moscow, in 1990 and 1991, packs of Marlboro cigarettes had attained the status of a kind of currency. People would accept payment in Marlboros, even though they did not themselves smoke. The combination of paper and tobacco already had an agentive function, named by the word "cigarette," and on top of that function was imposed the agentive function named by "medium of exchange."

The story told about medieval Europe is that bankers would accept gold and store it for safekeeping, and in return for the gold they issued paper certificates to the depositors of the gold. The certificates then could be used as a medium of exchange, just as the gold itself was. The certificate was a kind of substitute for the gold. It had complete credibility as an object of value, because at any point, it was exchangeable for gold. Commodity money had thus been replaced by contract money.

A stroke of genius occurred when somebody figured out that we can increase the supply of money simply by issuing more certificates than we have gold. As long as the certificates continue to function, as long as they have a collectively imposed function that continues to be collectively accepted, the certificates are, as they say, as good as gold. The next stroke of genius came when somebody figured out—and it took a long time for people to figure this out—we can forget about the gold and just have the certificates. With this change we have arrived at fiat money, and that is the situation we are in today. On old Federal Reserve notes it said we could take the bill to the Treasury and they would "pay the bearer" the equivalent in "dollars." But suppose we gave them a twenty dollar Federal Reserve note, what exactly would they give us? Another twenty dollar Federal Reserve note![5]

Constitutive Rules: X counts as Y in C

I think we can better understand what is going on in the evolution of money if we explore the relation of constitutive rules to the creation of institutional facts. I said that the form of the constitutive rule was "X counts as Y in C"; but as I am using this locution, that only determines a set of institutional facts and institutional objects where the Y term names something more than the sheer physical features of the object named by the X term.[6] Furthermore, the "counts as" locution names a feature of the imposition of a status to which a function is attached by way of collective intentionality, where the status and its accompanying function go beyond the sheer brute physical functions that can be assigned to physical objects. So, for example, as I am using this formula, it would not be a statement of a constitutive rule to say "objects that are designed and used to be sat on by one person count as chairs," because satisfying the X term is already sufficient for satisfying the Y term, just from the definition of the word "chair." The "rule" does not add anything but a label, so it is not a constitutive rule. Furthermore, it does not express a constitutive rule to say "objects of a certain shape count as chairs," because the functions assigned can be assigned independently of any human agreement. If it has a certain kind of shape, we can use it as a chair regardless of what anyone else thinks. But when we say that such and such bits of paper count as money, we genuinely have a constitutive rule, because satisfying the X term, "such and such bits of paper," is not by itself sufficient for being money, nor does the X term specify causal features that would be sufficient to enable the stuff to function as money without human agreement. So the application of the constitutive rule introduces the following features: The Y term has to assign a new *status* that the object does not already have just in virtue of satisfying the X term; and there has to be collective agreement, or at least acceptance, both in the imposition of that status on the stuff referred to by the X term and about the function that goes with that status. Furthermore, because the physical features specified by the X term are insufficient by themselves to guarantee the fulfillment of the assigned function specified by the Y term, the new status and its attendant functions have to be the sort of things that can be constituted by collective agreement or acceptance.

Also, because the physical features specified by the X term are insufficient to guarantee success in fulfilling the assigned function, there must be *continued* collective acceptance or recognition of the validity of the assigned function; otherwise the function cannot be successfully performed. It is not enough, for example, that we agree with the original assignment, "This stuff is money"; we must continue to accept it as money or it will become worthless.

Our sense that there is an element of magic, a conjuring trick, a sleight of hand in the creation of institutional facts out of brute facts derives from the nonphysical, noncausal character of the relation of the X and Y terms in the structure where we simply *count* X things as Y things. In our toughest metaphysical moods we want to ask "But is an X really a Y?" For example, are these bits of paper really *money?* Is this piece of land really somebody's *private property?* Is making certain noises in a ceremony really *getting married?* Even, is making noises through the mouth really making a *statement* or a *promise?* Surely when you get down to brass tacks, these are not real facts. We do not have this sense of giddiness where the agentive function is performed entirely in virtue of physical features. Thus, we do not have any metaphysical doubts about whether or not this is really a screwdriver, or this is really a car, because the sheer physical features of the objects in question enable them to function as screwdrivers or cars.

At this point I am simply describing the structure whereby institutional reality actually works in real human societies. Because this step is crucial for my argument, I will go through it slowly, using the example of U.S. paper money; and since I hope to be able to generalize certain features of the example, I will list its most salient general characteristics. Certain sorts of bits of paper are widely circulated in the United States. These pieces of paper satisfy certain conditions that constitute satisfying the X term. The pieces must have particular material ingredients, and they must match a certain set of patterns (five dollar bill, ten dollar bill, etc.).

They must also be issued by the Bureau of Engraving and Printing under the authority of the U.S. Treasury. Anything that satisfies these conditions (X term) counts as money, i.e., U.S. paper currency (Y term). But to describe these bits of paper with the Y term "money" does more than provide a shorthand label for the features of the X term; it describes a new status, and that status, viz. money, has a set of functions attached to it, e.g., medium of exchange, store of value, etc. In virtue of the constitutive rule, the paper counts as "legal tender for all debts public and private." And the imposition of this status function by the Y term has to be collectively recognized and accepted or the function will not be performed.

Some of the most salient generalizable features of this example are as follows:

First, collective intentionality assigns a new status to some phenomenon, where that status has an accompanying function that cannot be performed solely in virtue of the intrinsic physical features of the phenomenon in question. This assignment creates a new fact, an institutional fact, a new fact created by human agreement.

Second, the *form* of the assignment of the new status function can be represented by the formula "X counts as Y in C." This formula gives us a powerful tool for understanding the form of the creation of the new institutional fact, because the form of the collective intentionality is to impose that status and its function, specified by the Y term, on some phenomenon named by the X term. The "counts as" locution is crucial in this formula because since the function in question cannot be performed solely in virtue of the physical features of the X element, it requires our agreement or acceptance that it be performed. Thus, we agree to count the object named by the X term as having the status and function specified by the Y term. The sorts of functions and statuses that can be assigned by the Y term, therefore, are seriously limited by the possibilities of having functions where the performance of the function contains an element that can be guaranteed simply by collective agreement or acceptance. This is, perhaps, the most mysterious feature of institutional facts, and I will have a good deal to say about it later.

Third, the process of the creation of institutional facts may proceed without the participants being conscious that it is happening according to this form. The evolution may be such that the participants think, e.g., "I can exchange this for gold," "This is valuable," or even simply "This is money." They need not think, "We are collectively imposing a value on something that we do not regard as valuable because of its purely physical features," even though that is exactly what they are doing. There are two points about the relation of this process to consciousness. First, obviously, for most institutions we simply grow up in a culture where we take the institution for granted. We need not be consciously aware of its ontology. But second, and more to the point here, in the very evolution of the institution the participants need not be consciously aware of the form of the collective intentionality by which they are imposing functions on objects. In the course of consciously buying, selling, exchanging, etc., they may simply evolve institutional facts. Furthermore, in extreme cases they may accept the imposition of function only because of some related theory, which may not even be true. They may believe that it is money only if it is "backed by gold" or that it is a marriage only if it is sanctified by God or that so and so is the king only because he is divinely authorized. Throughout the history of the United States, literally millions of Americans have thought that the Constitution was divinely inspired. As long as people continue to recognize the X as having the Y status function, the institutional fact is created and maintained. They do not in addition have to recognize that they are so recognizing, and they may hold all sorts of other false beliefs about what they are doing and why they are doing it.

FOURTH, where the imposition of status function according to the formula becomes a matter of general policy, the formula acquires a normative status. It becomes a constitutive *rule*. This is shown by the fact that the general rule creates the possibility of abuses that could not exist without the rule, such as counterfeit money (objects are designed to look as if they satisfy the X term, when they do not) and hyperinflation (too much money is issued, so that the objects satisfying the X term can no longer perform the function specified by the Y term). The possibility of such forms of abuse is characteristic of institutional facts. Thus, for example, the fact that attorneys have to be certified creates the possibility that those who are not certified can pretend that they are and thus pretend that they are attorneys. They are, so to speak, "counterfeit" attorneys. But even a person qualified as an attorney can abuse the position and so fail to perform the functions properly (malpractice). Another illustration is provided by the decay of the institution of knighthood during the Middle Ages. At first knights were required to be competent warriors, in charge of many men and owning a lot of horses, etc. When decay set in, many people who did not meet the criteria (X term) for becoming knights asked the king to make them knights (Y term) anyway. Though they didn't pass the tests, they, for example, insisted that because they came from such a good family, the requirements should be waived in their case. Furthermore, many people who did rightfully acquire the status of knight became unable to carry out the functions of knighthood. They no longer had the required number of horses, or the required sort of armor, or they were not in the physical condition necessary to carry out the tasks of knighthood.

Where money is concerned cultures vary with their emphasis on the X or the Y aspect. United States currency is explicit on the Y aspect. It says, "This note is legal tender for all debts public and private," but it says nothing about counterfeiting. French currency, on the other hand, contains a long statement about the X aspect, specifically about the illegality of and punishment for counterfeiting.* Italian currency makes the same X aspect point, but more succinctly: "La legge punisce i fabbricatore e gli spacciatori di biglietti falsi."

FIFTH, the relation of rule and convention, at least in this case, is reasonably clear. That objects can function as a medium of exchange is not a matter of convention but of rule. But *which objects* perform this function is a matter of convention. Analogously, in chess, the powers of the king are not a matter of convention but of rule. But *which shape* to impose those powers on is a matter of convention. Because in these cases the conditions laid down by the X term are only incidentally related to the function specified by the Y term, the selection of the X term is more or less arbitrary; and the resulting policy as to which types of things shall be used as, e.g., money or a king in chess, is a matter of convention. As we will see in later examples, often the features necessary for the applicability of the X term are essential to the performance of the Y term. Thus, for example, when it comes to being a certified surgeon, the authorization to perform surgery (Y term) has to be based on meeting certain medical criteria (X term). Nonetheless, even in these cases, there is an addition marked by the Y term that is not already present in the X term. The person in question now has the status, e.g., of certified surgeon.

It might seem that there are obvious counterexamples to the claim that the features of the X term are insufficient to guarantee the function named by the Y term. For example, when the president or a state governor declares an earthquake or a major fire to be a "disaster," surely, one might say, the brute facts about the

---

*L'article 139 du code pénal punit de la réclusion criminelle a perpétuité ceux qui auront contrefait ou falsifié les billets de banque autorisés par la loi, ainsi ce que ceux qui auront fait usage de ces billets contrefaits ou falsifié, ceux qui les auront introduits en France seront punis de la même peine.

earthquake or fire are sufficient to qualify them as disasters in virtue of their physical features. There is nothing conventional about being an earthquake or a holocaust. But if one looks closely at these cases, even they illustrate the point. The function of a declared disaster is that the local victims qualify for such things as financial aid and low-interest loans, whereas fires and earthquakes by themselves do not generate money in virtue of their brute physical features and consequences.

A similar point can be made about the criminal law. The whole point of the criminal law is regulative, not constitutive. The point is to forbid, for example, certain antecedently existing forms of behavior such as killing. But to make the regulations work, there must be sanctions, and that requires the imposition of a new status on the person who violates the law. Thus the person who kills another (X term), under certain circumstances (C term), and is found guilty of so doing is now assigned the status of "convicted murderer" (Y term, and hence, institutional fact); and with that new status come the appropriate punishments. Thus the regulative "Thou shalt not kill" generates the appropriate constitutive "Killing, under certain circumstances, counts as murder, and murder counts as a crime punishable by death or imprisonment."

In many cases the X term is chosen precisely because it is supposed to have the features necessary to perform the function specified by the Y term. Thus, for example, each of the expressions "attorney," "physician," "president," and "cathedral" names a status with a function imposed on entities—graduates of law school or medical school, winners of certain sorts of elections, and large buildings capable of accommodating big church services and acting as the seat of a bishopric—precisely because they are supposed to be able to perform the Y functions implied by the status labels "attorney," "physician," "president," or "cathedral." But even in these cases, something is added by the Y term. The features specified by the X term are not themselves enough to guarantee the additional status and function specified by the Y term. The difference between attorneys and screwdrivers, for example, is that the screwdriver just has the sheer physical structure to enable it to perform its function, but for the law school graduate to be an attorney, an additional authorization or certification is required to confer the status of attorney. Collective agreement about the possession of the status is constitutive of having the status, and having the status is essential to the performance of the function assigned to that status.

An interesting class of cases are those where the entity in question has *both* a causal agentive function and correlated status-function. Consider, for example, the actual fence on portions of the border between Mexico and the United States. It is supposed to function causally as a physical barrier to crossing the border. But it is also supposed to mark a national boundary, something one is not supposed to cross unless authorized. Even in this case the status-function is in addition to the physical function, even though they both have the same ultimate objective.

The point is that the Y term must assign some new status that the entities named by the X term do not already have, and this new status must be such that human agreement, acceptance, and other forms of collective intentionality are necessary and sufficient to create it. Now, you might think, that is not much of an apparatus to work with, but in fact, as we will see in detail, the mechanism is a powerful engine in the generation of social reality.

SIXTH, finally there is a special relation between the imposition of these status-functions and language. The labels that are a part of the Y expression, such as the label "money," are now partly constitutive of the fact created. Odd as it may sound, in the creation of money, the linguistically expressed concepts, such as "money," are now parts of the very facts we have created. I will explore this feature in the next chapter.

Why Self-Referentiality Does Not
Result in Circularity

In my list of six apparent features of social reality that needed explanation, the first was a puzzle about how we can define "money," if part of the definition is "being thought of, or regarded as, or believed to be money." I asked: does this not lead to a circularity or infinite regress in any attempt to define the word, or even to give an explanation of the concept of money? But the resolution of the paradox is quite simple. The word "money" marks one node in a whole network of practices, the practices of owning, buying, selling, earning, paying for services, paying off debts, etc. As long as the object is regarded as having that role in the practices, we do not actually need the word "money" in the definition of money, so there is no circularity or infinite regress. The word "money" functions as a placeholder for the linguistic articulation of all these practices. To believe that something is money, one does not actually need the word "money." It is sufficient that one believes that the entities in question are media of exchange, repositories of value, payment for debts, salaries for services rendered, etc. And what goes for money goes for other institutional notions such as marriage, property, and speech acts such as promising, stating, ordering, etc. In short, the fact that a set of attitudes is partly constitutive of the truth conditions of a certain concept, and the fact that those attitudes would normally be summarized by using that very concept (e.g., thinking that something is money, thinking that those people are married), does not have the consequence that the word expressing that concept cannot be defined without circularity or infinite regress.

Although we do not need the concept "money" to define "money," and thus we avoid an immediate circularity, to explain the concept we do need other institutional concepts such as "buying," "selling," and "owing," and thus we avoided the vicious circularity only by expanding the circle by including other institutional concepts. We are not trying to reduce the concept "money" to noninstitutional concepts.

I mentioned that there is a distinction between the self-referentiality of the concept as applied to types and as applied to tokens. Where money is concerned a particular token could be money even if no one thought it was money, but where cocktail parties are concerned if no one thinks of a particular event that it is a cocktail party, it is not a cocktail party. I think the reason we treat cocktail parties differently from money in this regard has to do with codification. In general, if the institution in question is codified in an "official" form, such as in the laws concerning money, then the self-referentiality in question is a feature of the type. If it is informal, uncodified, then the self-referentiality applies to each token. Codification specifies the features a token must have in order to be an instance of the type. Hence a token may have those features even if no one thinks about it, but the type is still defined in this self-referential way.

The self-referentiality we have been discussing is an immediate consequence of the nature of agentive functions. It is not peculiar to institutional facts. So, for example, in order that something be a chair, it has to function as a chair, and hence, it has to be thought of or used as a chair. Chairs are not abstract or symbolic in the way that money and property are, but the point is the same in both cases. Where agentive functional concepts are concerned, part of satisfying a description is being thought to satisfy that description. This does not lead to circularity or infinite regress for the reason just stated: We can cash out the description in terms of the set of practices in which the phenomenon is embedded. Chairs are for sitting in, money is to buy things with, tools are for manipulating objects in various ways, etc.*

---

*In the *Random House Dictionary*, one of the definitions given for "tool" is: "anything that can be used as tool." As a definition, that seems pretty dumb, but it is not quite as dumb as it looks. You could not define "screwdriver" as "anything that can be used as a screwdriver," because lots of things can be used as screw-

The Use of Performative Utterances in the Creation of Institutional Facts

The second apparent feature we need to explain concerns the role of performative utterances in the creation of many, though not all, institutional facts. The explanation is provided by the structure of constitutive rules. *In general, where the X term is a speech act, the constitutive rule will enable the speech act to be performed as a performative declaration creating the state of affairs described by the Y term.* Because saying certain things *counts as* entering into a contract or adjourning a meeting, you can perform those acts by saying you are performing them. If you are the chairman, then saying in appropriate circumstances "The meeting is adjourned" will make it the case that the meeting is adjourned. Saying, in appropriate circumstances, "I appoint you chairman" will make it the case that you are chairman. The same words said by the wrong person or in the wrong circumstances will have no such effect. Because the constitutive rule enables the function to be imposed on a speech act, then just performing that speech act in appropriate circumstances can constitute the imposition of that function, and thus will constitute a new institutional fact.

It is said that in Moslem countries a man can divorce his wife by simply saying "I divorce you" three times while throwing three white pebbles. This is clearly a performative use of the verb "divorce," which does not exist in other countries. Those who think that meaning is use would have to conclude that the word "divorce" has a different meaning for Moslems than it does for others. But that is not the case. What has happened is that a new status-function has been imposed on an existing sentence form. The sentence form "I divorce you" does not change its meaning when a new status-function is added; rather, it is now simply used

---

drivers that definitely are not screwdrivers, for instance, coins. But since "tool," unlike "screwdriver," names a very large class of agentive functions, anything that can be used as a tool is, roughly speaking, a tool.

in the creation of a new institutional fact, namely, the particular divorce, in virtue of a new constitutive rule according to which the husband's saying "I divorce you" three times with the appropriate throwing gestures counts as divorcing his wife. Thus the performative utterance creates a new institutional fact, the divorce.

Even the statement on the twenty dollar bill, though it contains no performative verbs, is a declaration. It says, "This note is legal tender for all debts, public and private." But that utterance is not an empirical claim. It will not do, for example, to ask the Treasury, "How do you know it is legal tender?" or "What's the evidence?" When the Treasury says it is legal tender, they are *declaring* it to be legal tender, not announcing an empirical fact that it already is legal tender.

The possibility of creating institutional facts by declaration does not hold for every institutional fact. You cannot, for example, make a touchdown just by saying you are making it.

To summarize this point: performatives play a special role in the creation of institutional facts, because the status-function marked by the Y term in the formula "X counts as Y" can often, though not always, be imposed simply by declaring it to be imposed. This is especially true where the X term is itself a speech act.

The Logical Priority of Brute Facts over Institutional Facts

The third apparent feature we need to explain concerns the priority of brute facts over institutional facts. As with feature two, this is explained by the structure of constitutive rules. The structure of institutional facts is the structure of hierarchies of the form "X counts as Y in context C." That hierarchy has to bottom out in phenomena whose existence is not a matter of human agreement. This is just another way of saying that where there is a status-function imposed on something, there has to be something it is imposed on. If it is imposed on another status-function, eventually one has to reach a rock bottom of something that is not itself any form of status-function. So, for example, as I said earlier, all sorts of things can be money, but there has to be some physical realization, some brute fact—even if it is only a bit of paper or a blip on a computer disk—on which we can impose our institutional form of status function. Thus there are no institutional facts without brute facts.

This discussion anticipates a discussion of realism I will present in Chapters 7 and 8. It could not be the case, as some antirealists have maintained, that all facts are institutional facts, that there are no brute facts, because the analysis of the structure of institutional facts reveals that they are logically dependent on brute facts. To suppose that all facts are institutional would produce an infinite regress or circularity in the account of institutional facts. In order that some facts be institutional, there must be some other facts that are brute. This is a consequence of the logical structure of institutional facts.

Systematic Relations and the Primacy of the Act over the Object

Our fourth question was, Why are there always certain sorts of systematic relations among institutional facts? And the fifth was, Why do institutional acts seem prior to institutional objects?

The most obvious reason why there are systematic relationships among the various sorts of social facts of the type that I tried to describe is that the facts in question are designed for precisely that purpose. Governments are designed to impact on our lives in all sorts of ways; money is designed to provide a unit of value in all kinds of transactions. Even games, which are explicitly designed to be insulated from the rest of our lives, nonetheless employ an apparatus—of rights, obligations, responsibilities, etc.—that, as I remarked earlier, is intelligible only given all sorts of other social facts.

The explanation for the apparent primacy of social acts over so-

cial objects is that the "objects" are really designed to serve agentive functions, and have little interest for us otherwise. What we
think of as social *objects*, such as governments, money, and universities, are in fact just placeholders for patterns of *activities*. I
hope it is clear that the whole operation of agentive functions and
collective intentionality is a matter of ongoing activities and the
creation of the possibility of more ongoing activities.

Unconsciously, we have throughout this discussion been ac-
knowledging this point by our talk of institutional *facts* rather than
institutional *objects*. Such material objects as are involved in institutional reality, e.g., bits of paper, are objects like any others, but
the imposition of status-functions on these objects creates a level
of description of the object where it is an institutional object, e.g., a
twenty dollar bill. The object is no different; rather, a new status
with an accompanying function has been assigned to an old object
(or a new object has been created solely for the purpose of serving
the new status-function), but that function is manifested only in actual transactions; hence, our interest is not in the object but in the
processes and events where the functions are manifested.

The priority of process over product also explains why, as several social theorists have pointed out, institutions are not worn
out by continued use, but each use of the institution is in a sense
a renewal of that institution. Cars and shirts wear out as we use
them but constant use renews and strengthens institutions such
as marriage, property, and universities. The account I have given
explains this fact: since the function is imposed on a phenomenon
that does not perform that function solely in virtue of its physical
construction, but in terms of the continued collective intentionality of the users, each use of the institution is a renewed expression
of the commitment of the users to the institution. Individual dollar bills wear out. But the institution of paper currency is rein-
forced by its continual use.

The sixth and final feature we need to explain concerns the role
of language in institutional reality, and to that topic I devote the
next chapter.

3
Language and Social Reality

The primary aim of this chapter is to explain and justify my claim that language is essentially constitutive of institutional reality. I have made this claim in general terms but I now want to make fully explicit what I mean by it, and to present arguments for it. At the end of the chapter I will mention some other functions of language in institutional facts.

I said in the last chapter that it seems impossible to have institutional structures such as money, marriage, governments, and property without some form of language because, in some weird sense I have not yet explained, the words or other symbols are partly constitutive of the facts. But this will seem puzzling when we reflect that social facts in general do not require language. Prelinguistic animals can have all sorts of cooperative behavior, and human infants are clearly capable of interacting socially in quite complex ways without any words. Furthermore, if we are going to say that institutional reality requires language, what

59

about language itself? If institutional facts require language and language is itself an institution, then it seems language must require language, and we have either infinite regress or circularity.

There is a weaker and a stronger version of my claim. The weaker is that in order to have institutional facts at all, a society must have at least a primitive form of a language, that in this sense the institution of language is logically prior to other institutions. On this view language is the basic social institution in the sense that all others presuppose language, but language does not presuppose the others: you can have language without money and marriage, but not the converse. The stronger claim is that each institution requires linguistic elements of the facts within that very institution. I believe both claims are true, and I will be arguing for the stronger claim. The stronger claim implies the weaker.

Language-Dependent Thoughts and Language-Dependent Facts

To explain the issues and the arguments I will be presenting, I need to make, if only briefly, certain elementary clarifications and distinctions. I need to make explicit which features of language are relevant to this issue. I will not attempt to define "language" here, and many features that are essential to full-blown natural languages—such as infinite generative capacity, the presence of illocutionary force indicating devices, quantifiers, and logical connectives—are irrelevant to this discussion. The feature of language essential for the constitution of institutional facts is the existence of symbolic devices, such as words, that by convention *mean* or *represent* or *symbolize* something beyond themselves. So when I say that language is partly constitutive of institutional facts, I do not mean that institutional facts require full-blown natural languages like French, German, or English. My claim that language is partly constitutive of institutional facts amounts to the claim that institutional facts essentially contain some symbolic elements in this sense of "symbolic": there are words, symbols, or other *conventional* devices that *mean* something or express something or represent or symbolize something beyond themselves, *in a way that is publicly understandable.* I want that to sound very vague and general at this point, because it is, so far, designed only to specify the feature of language that I want to claim has a constitutive role in institutional reality.

Language, as I am using the notion here, essentially contains entities that symbolize; and in language, as opposed to prelinguistic intentional states, such intentionalistic capacities are not intrinsic to the entities but are imposed by or derived from the intrinsic intentionality of humans. Thus the sentence "I am hungry" is part of language because it has representational or symbolic capacities by convention. But the actual feeling of hunger is not part of language because it represents its conditions of satisfaction intrinsically. You do not need language or any other sorts of conventions to feel hungry.

We need first to distinguish between *language-independent facts,* such as the fact that Mt. Everest has snow and ice at the summit, and *language-dependent facts,* such as the fact that "Mt. Everest has snow and ice at the summit" is a sentence of English. Though there are no doubt marginal cases, the principle is clear enough—a fact is language independent if that very fact requires no linguistic elements for its existence. Take away all language and Mt. Everest still has snow and ice near the summit; take away all language and you have taken away the fact that "Mt. Everest has snow and ice at the summit" is a sentence of English.

A second distinction we need is between *language-dependent thoughts* and *language-independent thoughts.* Some thoughts are language dependent in the sense that an animal could not have that very thought if the animal did not have words or some other linguistic devices for thinking that very thought, but some thoughts are language independent in the sense that an animal can have those thoughts without having words or any other linguistic devices. An obvious case of a language-dependent thought is the thought that "Mt. Everest has snow and ice at the summit" is a sentence of English. A being that did not have a language could not think that thought. The most obvious cases of language-independent thoughts are noninstitutional, primitive, biological inclinations and cognitions not requiring any linguistic devices. For example, an animal can have conscious feelings of hunger and thirst and each of these is a form of desire. Hunger is a desire to eat and thirst a desire to drink, and desires are intentional states with full intentional contents; in the contemporary jargon, they are "propositional attitudes." Furthermore, an animal can have prelinguistic perceptions and prelinguistic beliefs derived from these perceptions. My dog can see and smell a cat run up a tree and form the belief that the cat is up the tree. He can even correct the belief and form a new belief when he sees and smells that the cat has run into the neighbor's yard. Other cases of prelinguistic thoughts are emotions such as fear and rage. We ought to allow ourselves to be struck both by the fact that animals can have prelinguistic thoughts and by the fact that some thoughts are language dependent and cannot be had by prelinguistic beings.

With these distinctions in mind, let us restate the thesis we are trying to examine. I have argued that some facts that do not on the surface appear to be language dependent—facts about money and property, for example—are in fact language dependent. But how could they be language dependent since, unlike English sentences, money and property are not words nor are they composed of words?

It is a sufficient condition for a *fact* to be language dependent that two conditions be met. First, mental representations, such as thoughts, must be partly constitutive of the fact; and second, the representations in question must be language dependent. It follows immediately from the structure of constitutive rules that the first of these conditions is met by institutional facts. From the fact that the status function specified by the Y term can be fulfilled only if it is recognized, accepted, acknowledged, or otherwise believed in, it follows that the institutional fact in question can exist only if it is represented as existing. Ask yourself what must be the case in order that it be true that the piece of paper in my hand is a twenty dollar bill or that Tom owns a house, and you will see that there must be mental representations as partly constitutive of these facts. These facts can exist only if people have certain sorts of beliefs and other mental attitudes. This is what I was driving at earlier when I said that a type of thing is money only if people believe it is money, something is property only if people believe it is property. All institutional facts are, in this sense, ontologically subjective, even though in general they are epistemically objective.

But what about the second condition? Must the representations in question be language dependent? The satisfaction of the first condition does not by itself entail the satisfaction of the second. A fact could contain mental states as constitutive features and still not be linguistic. For example, suppose we arbitrarily create a word "dogbone" to mean a bone desired by at least one dog. Then the fact that such and such is a dogbone is in part constituted by some canine mental state. But there is nothing necessarily linguistic about such mental states, because dogs can desire bones without any language in which to express the desire.

So what is the difference between dogbones and money, for example? Why does the belief that something is money require language for its very existence in the way that the desire for a bone does not? What exactly must happen in order for me to think, "This is money"? We saw in Chapter 2 that I do not need the word "money" itself, so the word does not have to figure in its own definition. But why do I still have to have some words or wordlike elements to think the thoughts? This is not a trivial question. The answer to it can derive only from the character of the move from X to Y when we count some X as having the status-function named by the Y term. The answer, in short, must come from an understanding of the nature of status-functions. The answer I will give, to anticipate a bit, is that the move from X to Y is *eo ipso* a linguistic move, even in cases that apparently have nothing to do with language.

Why Are Any Thoughts Language Dependent?

Our original thesis, that institutional facts are language dependent, boils down to the thesis that the thoughts that are constitutive of institutional facts are language dependent. But why? What is the argument? Let's begin by asking, why are *any* thoughts, other than thoughts about linguistic elements themselves, language dependent? There are different sorts of cases.

First, some thoughts are of such complexity that it would be *empirically impossible* to think them without being in possession of symbols. Mathematical thoughts, for example, require a system of symbols. It would be extremely difficult and probably impossible for a prelinguistic beast to think even such a simple arithmetical thought as that

$$371 + 248 = 619.$$

But these are cases of empirical difficulty. Because of the way we are constituted, complex abstract thoughts require words and symbols. I see no *logical* impossibility in thinking such a thought without language. It is easy to imagine that the course of evolution might produce beings who can think of complex arithmetical relations without using symbols.

Another sort of case involves language as a matter of *logical necessity*, because the linguistic expression of the thought is essential to its being the thought that it is. For example, consider the thought "Today is Tuesday the 26th of October." Such a thought requires a quite definite set of words or their synonyms in English and other languages because the content of the thought locates a day in relation to a specific verbal system for identifying days and months. That is why my dog cannot think "Today is Tuesday the 26th of October."

We who are in possession of the relevant vocabulary can translate the expression "Tuesday the 26th of October" into French but not into another radically different calendar, such as the Mayan. The Mayans, using their system, could have identified an actual day we call "Tuesday the 26th of October," but their thought does not translate into "Tuesday the 26th of October." Same reference, different sense.

The thought is language dependent because the corresponding fact is language dependent. There is no fact of the matter about its being Tuesday the 26th of October except the fact that it occupies a position relative to a verbal system. "But," one might say, "exactly the same is true of, for example, dogs and cats. Something is correctly called a 'dog' or a 'cat' only relative to a linguistic system. Something is a dog only relative to a system for identifying animals and objects generally." There is this crucial difference: The features that an object has *in virtue of which the word "dog" is true of it, i.e., the features in virtue of which it is a dog, are features that exist independently of language.* And to the extent that one can think of those features independently of a language, one can have that thought independently of language. But the features in virtue of which today is Tuesday the 26th of October cannot exist independently of a verbal system, because its being Tuesday the 26th of October is a matter of its relation to a verbal system. If there were no verbal system, there would be no such fact, even though this day remains the day that it is regardless of what anybody thinks or says. In short, this thought is language dependent because part of the content of the thought is that this day satisfies conditions that exist only relative to words.

The fact that today is Tuesday the 26th of October is not an institutional fact because, though the day is institutionally identified as such, no new status-function is carried by the label.* Now let us consider institutional facts. I am claiming that the thoughts that this is a twenty dollar bill and that this is my property require a language as a matter of conceptual necessity. I am claiming that

---

*Some names for dates are labels for status-functions, for example, "Christmas," or "Thanksgiving." Such labels do more than identify a day relative to a verbal system; they also assign a status to which functions attach.

such thoughts are like thoughts about today's date in that they are essentially language dependent. Why?

Games and Institutional Reality

To argue for this claim, I want to begin by considering some fairly simple facts regarding games, because they illustrate the points I want to make. Consider the case of points scored in a game such as football. We say "a touchdown counts six points." Now, that is not a thought that anyone could have without linguistic symbols. But, to repeat, why? Because points can exist only relative to a linguistic system for representing and counting points, and thus we can think about points only if we are in possession of the linguistic apparatus necessary for such a system. But that pushes the question further back. Why can points exist only relative to such a linguistic system? The answer, to put it simply, is that if you take away all the symbolic devices for representing points, there is nothing else there. There is just the system for representing and counting points. That would be misleading if it gave us the impression that points are just words. That is not right. The words have consequences. People try desperately hard to score points in a way they would not try for mere words, because the points determine victory and defeat, and thus are the occasion of emotions ranging from ecstasy to despair. Mere words, it seems, could not be the focus of such deep feelings. But there is no thought independent of the words or other symbols to the effect that we have scored six points. The points might be represented by some symbolic devices other than actual words, for example, we might count points by assembling piles of stones, one stone for each point. But then the stones would be as much linguistic symbols as would any others. They would have the three essential features of linguistic symbols: they *symbolize* something beyond themselves, they do so by *convention*, and they are *public*.

There are no prelinguistic perceptions of points, nor prelinguistic beliefs about points, because there is nothing there to perceive or have beliefs about except the relevant symbolic devices. The animal cannot prelinguistically see points the way it can see the cat up the tree, nor can it prelinguistically desire points the way it desires food.

But why could an animal not just be born with a prelinguistic desire to score points in football games as animals are born with prelinguistic desires to drink their mother's milk? The answer is that the desire to score points has no content independently of a socially accepted system of representing and counting points. Take away all symbolic systems for counting points and you have taken away all possible beliefs, desires, and thoughts generally about points. Later I will argue that what is true of points in football games is true of money, property, and other institutional phenomena.

Our difficulty in seeing these facts derives in part from a certain model we have of how language works. The model works for a large number of cases and therefore we think it must work in all cases. Here is the model: There are words and other expressions, these have senses or meanings, and in virtue of these senses they have referents. For example, there is an expression "The Evening Star"; it has a sense or meaning; in virtue of that meaning, when we think or utter the expression we refer to or think about the language-independent object, the Evening Star. On this model, if you can think the sense or meaning without the words, then you can think of the referent without the words. All you have to do is detach the sense or meaning from the expression and just think the sense or meaning. And it seems we must *always* be able to detach the meaning because we can translate the expression into other languages, and this translatability seems to prove that there is a detachable, thinkable sense that can attach now to English now to German words, etc. The model gives us the impression that there are no such things as thoughts that are necessarily language dependent, because it seems any expression in any language can be translated into other languages, and this seems to imply that the thinkable sense is always detachable from the speakable or writable expression.

Whatever its other limitations, this model does not work for institutional facts. In the case of scoring points in games, we can see clearly why it does not work. Even if we don't have words for "man," "line," "ball," etc., we can see that man cross that line carrying that ball, and thus we can think a thought without words, which thought we would report in the words "The man crossed the line carrying the ball." But we cannot in addition see the man score six points because there is nothing in addition to see. The expression "six points" does not refer to some language-independent objects in the way that the expressions "the man," "the ball," "the line," and "The Evening Star" refer to language-independent objects. Points are not "out there" in the way that planets, men, balls, and lines are out there.

I hope the reader shares my intuitions so far, because I now want to state the general principle that underlies them. At the lowest level, the shift from the X to the Y in the move that creates institutional facts is a move from a brute level to an institutional level. That shift, as I have emphasized over and over, can exist only if it is represented as existing. But there can be no prelinguistic way to represent the Y element because there is nothing there prelinguistically that one can perceive or otherwise attend to in addition to the X element, and there is nothing there prelinguistically to be the target of desire or inclination in addition to the X element. Without a language, we can see the man cross a white line holding a ball, and without language we can want a man to cross a white line holding a ball. But we cannot see the man score six points or want the man to score six points without language, because points are not something that can be thought of or that can exist independently of words or other sorts of markers. And what is true of points in games is true of money, governments, private property, etc., as we will see.

The lessons from this example can now be extended to institutional facts in general. The very design of status-functions is such that they both are partly constituted by thoughts and that prelinguistic forms of thought are inadequate to do the job. The reason is that they exist only by way of collective agreement, and there can be no prelinguistic way of formulating the content of the agreement, because there is no prelinguistic natural phenomenon there. The Y term creates a status that is additional to the physical features of the X term, and that status has to provide reasons for action that are independent of our natural inclinations. The status exists only if people believe it exists, and the reasons function only if people accept them as reasons. Therefore, the agent must have some way to represent the new status. He cannot do it in terms of prelinguistic brute features of the X term. He can't get from thoughts just about the color and the shape of the dollar bill to the status "money" any more than he can can get from thoughts just about the movement of the man with the ball to the status "touchdown, six points." Because the new status exists only by convention, there must be some conventional way to represent the status or the system will not work. "But why couldn't the X term itself be the conventional way to represent the new status?" The answer is that it could, *but to assign that role to the X term is precisely to assign it a symbolizing or linguistic status.*

Notice that status-functions differ from causal agentive functions in regard to their language dependency. One can think that this is a screwdriver without any words or other linguistic devices because one can just think that this thing is used to screw in these other things. No words at all are logically necessary to treat and use an object as a screwdriver because its ability to so function is a matter of its brute physical structure. But in the case of status-functions, there is no structural feature of the X element sufficient by itself to determine the Y function. Physically X and Y are exactly the same thing. The only difference is that we have imposed a status on the X element, and this new status needs *markers,* because, empirically speaking, there isn't anything else there.

To summarize: Because the Y level of the shift from X to Y in the creation of institutional facts has no existence apart from its representation, we need some way of representing it. But there is no natural prelinguistic way to represent it, because the Y element has no natural prelinguistic features in addition to the X element that would provide the means of representation. So we have to have words or other symbolic means to perform the shift from the X to the Y status.

I believe these points can be made clearer by calling attention to the deontic status of institutional phenomena. Animals running in a pack can have all the consciousness and collective intentionality they need. They can even have hierarchies and a dominant male; they can cooperate in the hunt, share their food, and even have pair bonding. But they cannot have marriages, property, or money. Why not? Because all these create institutional forms of powers, rights, obligations, duties, etc., and it is characteristic of such phenomena that they create reasons for action that are independent of what you or I or anyone else is otherwise inclined to do. Suppose I train my dog to chase dollar bills and bring them back to me in return for food. He still is not buying the food and the bills are not money to him. Why not? Because he cannot represent to himself the relevant deontic phenomena. He might be able to think "If I give him this he will give me that food." But he cannot think, for example, now I have the *right to buy* things and when someone else has this, he will also have the right to buy things.

Furthermore, such deontic phenomena are not reducible to something more primitive and simple. We cannot analyze or eliminate them in favor of dispositions to behave or fears of negative consequences of not doing something. Famously, Hume and many others have tried to make such eliminations, but without success.

I have argued in this chapter that institutional facts in general require language because the language is partly constitutive of the facts. But let us turn the question around. Could there be any institutional facts that are not language dependent, genuine facts satisfying our formula, X counts as Y, where the Y term imposes a new status by collective intentionality, but where the intentionality in question is not language dependent? Well, what about our first example of the physical barrier, the wall, that decays into a purely symbolic barrier, the line of stones? Isn't that an example of an institutional fact without language? This depends on how the tribe regards the line of stones. If, just as a matter of fact, they are not disposed to cross the line but just avoid crossing it out of habit, then they do not need a language for such a disposition. Prelinguistic animals, for example, can be trained not to cross certain boundaries, and many species of animals have natural ways, amazingly various, of marking territorial boundaries. As Broom writes, "The demarcation of a territory may be visual as in cleaner fish and other reef fish, auditory as in many birds, olfactory as in scent marking by many mammals, or electrical as in electric fish."[1] If our imagined tribe just is not disposed to cross the boundaries as a matter of inclination, they do not in our sense have an institutional fact. They simply have a disposition to behave in certain ways, and their behavior is just like the case of animals marking the limits of their territory. There is nothing deontic about such markings. The animals simply behave in such and such ways, and "behave" here means they simply move their bodies in specific ways.

But if we suppose that the members of the tribe recognize that the line of stones creates rights and obligations, that they are *forbidden* to cross the line, that they are *not supposed to* cross it, then we have symbolization. The stones now symbolize something beyond themselves; they function like words. I do not think there is a sharp dividing line between either the institutional and the noninstitutional or the linguistic and the prelinguistic, but to the extent that we think the phenomena are genuinely institutional facts, and not just conditioned forms of habitual behavior, to that very extent we must think of language as constitutive of the phenomena, because the move that imposes the Y function on the X object is a symbolizing move.

Does Language Require Language?

The account so far, however, seems to leave us in a fix. I have said that institutional facts require language because language is constitutive of the facts. But linguistic facts are also institutional facts. So it looks as if language requires language. Does this not lead to an infinite regress or another form of circularity? We got out of the first charge of circularity—the apparent circularity that defining institutional concepts such as "money" seemed to require those very concepts in the definition—by widening the circle to include other institutional concepts. How do we get out of this charge of circularity?

The short, but unsatisfactory-sounding, answer to this question is that language does not need language because it already is language. Now, let me explain what that means. The requirement that there be linguistic markers for institutional facts is the requirement that there be some conventional way for the participants in the institution to mark the fact that the X element now has the Y status. Since there is nothing in the physics of the X element that gives it the Y function, since the status is only by collective agreement, and since the status confers deontic properties that are not physical properties, the status cannot exist without markers. Those markers are now partly constitutive of the status. There needs to be some way to mark the fact that the man holding the ball has scored a touchdown, and that a touchdown counts six points. There is nothing in the physics of the situation that makes it apparent. And this is not an epistemic but an ontological point. Similarly, there is nothing in the physical relations between me and a piece of land that makes it my property. There is nothing in the chemical composition of this piece of paper that makes it a twenty dollar bill. So we have to have some symbolic devices for marking these institutional facts. But now, what about the symbolic devices themselves? How are they to be marked as symbolic? If it is true, as it surely is, that there is nothing in the physical structure of the piece of paper that makes it a five dollar bill, nothing in the physical structure of the piece of land that makes it my property, then it is also true that there is nothing in the acoustics of the sounds that come out of my mouth or the physics of the marks that I make on paper that makes them into words or other sorts of symbols.

The solution to our puzzle is to see that language is precisely designed to be a self-identifying category of institutional facts. The child is brought up in a culture where she learns to treat the sounds that come out of her own and others' mouths as standing for, or meaning something, or representing something. And this is what I was driving at when I said that language doesn't require language in order to be language because it already is language. But doesn't this only force our question back further? Why can't all institutional facts have this self-identifying character of language? Why can't the child just be brought up to regard this as so-and-so's private property, or this physical object as money? The answer is, she can. But precisely to the extent that she does, she is treating the object as symbolizing something beyond itself; she is treating it as at least partly linguistic in character.

The move from the brute to the institutional status is *eo ipso* a linguistic move, because the X term now symbolizes something beyond itself. But that symbolic move requires thoughts. In order to think the thought that constitutes the move from the X term to the Y status, there must be a vehicle of the thought. You have to have something to think with. The physical features of the X term are insufficient for the content of the thought, but any object whatever that can be conventionally used and thought of as the bearer of that content can be used to think the thought. The best objects to think with are words, because that is part of what words are for. Indeed, it is a condition for something to be a word that it be thinkable. But strictly speaking, any conventional marker will do. Though it is easy to think in words, it is hard to think in people, mountains, etc., because they have too many irrelevant features and they are too unmanageable. So we use real words or we can use wordlike markers as vehicles of thought. Using words, we say, "That is my property," "He is the chairman," etc. But words like "property" and "chairman" don't stand for prelinguistic objects in the way that "The Evening Star" stands for The Evening Star. Sometimes we put labels or symbols on the X element itself. The labels say, e.g., "This note is legal tender for all debts public and private." But that representation is now, at least in part, a declaration: it creates the institutional status by representing it as existing. It does not represent some prelinguistic natural phenomenon.

We can treat the X object itself as having the Y status by convention, as we can treat coins as money, or the line of stones as a boundary, but to do that is already to assign a linguistic status, because the objects now are conventional public symbols of something beyond themselves; they symbolize a deontic status beyond the physics. And all the cases I can think of where the X term is in this way self-identifying have the essential features of words: the type-token distinction applies, the X elements are readily recognizable, they are easily thinkable, and we see them as symbolizing the Y status by convention.

From the time of preliterate societies to the present, there have been lots of conventional markers that are not words but function just like words. Here are half a dozen examples: In the Middle Ages felons had their right palms branded to identify them as such. This is why we have to raise our right hand while taking an oath in court, so everybody can see that we are not felons. Priests had a bald spot shaved at the top of their head to mark the fact that they were priests. Kings wore crowns, husbands and wives wear wedding rings, cattle are branded, and lots of people wear uniforms as markers of their status.

The entire argument of this chapter has produced a strange result. I am not entirely comfortable with it, but here it is. The move from X to Y is already linguistic in nature because once the function is imposed on the X element, it now symbolizes something else, the Y function. This move can exist only if it is collectively represented as existing. The collective representation is public and conventional, and it requires some vehicle. Just scrutinizing or imaging the features of the X element will not do the job. So we need words, such as "money," "property," etc., or we need word-like symbols, such as those we just considered, or in the limiting case we treat the X elements themselves as *conventional representations* of the Y function. To the extent we can do that, they must be either words or symbols themselves or enough like words to be *both* bearers of the Y function and representations of the move from X to Y.

The account also has this consequence: the capacity to attach a sense, a symbolic function, to an object that does not have that sense intrinsically is the precondition not only of language but of all institutional reality. The preinstitutional capacity to symbolize is the condition of possibility of the creation of all human institutions. In certain contexts, uttering the sounds "the cat is on the mat" counts as making the statement that the cat is on the mat, and in certain contexts crossing the line while holding the ball counts as scoring a touchdown. Both are cases of the creation of institutional facts according to the formula. The difference in the two cases is that the creation of a speech act is the creation of something with further representational capacities, but in that sense points scored in games do not stand for something beyond themselves. Statements can be true or false, but touchdowns do not in that way have semantic properties.

Typically the "stands for" relation requires the existence of some object that exists independently of the symbol that stands for it, but in the case of institutional reality at the lowest level, the practice of attaching a sense to an object according to the constitutive rules creates the very category of potential referents. Symbols do not create cats and dogs and evening stars; they create only the possibility of referring to cats, dogs, and evening stars in a publicly accessible way. But symbolization creates the very ontological categories of money, property, points scored in games and political offices, as well as the categories of words, and speech acts. Once the categories are created, we can have the same sense/reference distinctions that we have for evening stars, etc.

Thus we can refer or fail to refer to "the touchdown we scored at the end of the fourth quarter" or "the President of the United States" in the same way we can succeed or fail to refer to "The Evening Star," but the difference is that the creation of the category of touchdowns and presidents is already achieved by the structures according to which we attach status-functions to the X terms, because the existence of these features is created by attachment of the status-functions.

Think of it this way: What stands to the sound "cat" as its meaning is what stands to the piece of paper as its function as a dollar bill. However, the sound "cat" has a *referential* function that the piece of paper does not have. For example, the sound can occur in sentences where the speaker in uttering the sentence refers to a cat. Pieces of paper, even pieces of paper construed as dollar bills, are not in that way used to refer. But the practice of using pieces of paper as dollar bills creates a class of entities that cannot exist without the practice. It creates the class of entities: dollar bills. In order that the practice should exist, people must be able to think the thought "This piece of paper is a dollar bill," and that is a thought they cannot think without words or other symbols, even if the only symbol in question is the object itself.

Other Functions of Language in Institutional Facts

This discussion has been very abstract and has concerned the conditions of the possibility of the creation of institutional reality, linguistic or otherwise. But if we consider actual natural languages such as French or German and the actual complexity of social institutions, we can see several other reasons why institutional facts require language.

First, language is epistemically indispensable.

I said that in the structure of institutional facts we impose a Y status-function on the X term, which it does not perform solely in virtue of its physical constitution. But now how are we to tell which entities have this status function imposed on them? For many causal agentive functions—not all—it is reasonably easy to tell which objects are chairs, tables, hammers, and screwdrivers because you can read off the function from the physical structure. But when it comes to money, husbands, university professors, and privately owned real estate, you cannot read off the function or status from the physics. You need labels. In order that we can *recognize* bits of paper as money, for example, we must have some linguistic or symbolic way of representing the newly created facts about functions, because they cannot be read off from the physics of the objects themselves. The recognition of the fact that something is money requires that it be linguistically or symbolically represented. I will have more to say about this feature in the next chapter, when we discuss what I call "status indicators."

Second, the facts in question, being inherently social, must be communicable.

If the systems are to function, then the newly created facts must be communicable from one person to another, even when invisible to the naked eye. You must be able to tell people that you are married, that you are the chairman, that the meeting is adjourned if the system is to function. Even in simple cases of institutional facts, this communicability requires a means of public communication, a language.

Third, in real life the phenomena in question are extremely complex, and the representation of such complex information requires language.

Even the most apparently simple act of buying and selling has great complexity, as we saw in our example of ordering beer in a café at the beginning of the book. Because the structure of the facts exists only to the extent that it is represented, complex facts require a complex system of representation for their existence; and such complex systems of representation are languages.

Fourth, the facts in question persist through time independently of the duration of the urges and inclinations of the participants in the institution.

This continued existence requires a means of representation of the facts that is independent of the more primitive prelinguistic psychological states of the participants, and such representations are linguistic.

4

The General Theory
of Institutional Facts

Part I: Iteration, Interaction, and Logical Structure

Generalizing the Analysis

So far I have given a preliminary account of institutional facts, using the example of money more than any other sort and emphasizing the special role of language in institutional reality. I will use the tools we have assembled to give an account that describes the structure not only of money but also of marriage, property, hiring, firing, war, revolutions, cocktail parties, governments, meetings, unions, parliaments, corporations, laws, restaurants, vacations, lawyers, professors, doctors, medieval knights, and taxes, for example. I do not know how to tell the story for each of these with the simplicity of the story about money. To generalize the account, we need to add at least two basic insights to the material of earlier chapters:

First, the structure "X counts as Y in C" can be iterated.

We can impose status-functions on entities that have already had status-functions imposed on them. In such cases the X term at a higher level can be a Y term from an earlier level. For example, only a citizen of the United States as X can become President as Y, but to be a citizen is to have a Y status-function from an earlier level. And we can impose status-functions where the C term determines a context that requires a previously imposed status-function. In such cases the C term at a higher level can be a Y term from an earlier level. For example, a marriage ceremony requires the presence of a presiding official as context C, but to be a presiding official is to have previously acquired a Y status-function. Furthermore, we can impose status-functions on entities whose previously imposed status-function was that of representing, i.e., we can impose them on speech acts. For example, a certain sort of promise as X can count as a contract Y, but to be a promise is already to have a Y status-function at a lower level. It is no exaggeration to say that these iterations provide the logical structure of complex societies.

Second, there can be interlocking systems of such iterated structures operating through time.

The structures of iterated status-functions do not just exist at instantaneous moments. The functions they perform require them to interact constantly with each other across extended periods. I do not, for example, just have *money*; rather, for example, I have *money* in my *bank account* that I *spend* by *writing a check* to *pay* my *state and federal taxes as a citizen of the United States* as well as a long-term *resident* and an *employee* of the *state of California*. All the italicized expressions in the previous sentence express institutional concepts, and the facts reported all presuppose systems of constitutive rules operating through time.

To develop the analysis further, let us try to tell a story about marriage and property analogous to the one we told about money. Such institutions originate in the sheer physical and intentional facts involved in cohabitation and physical possession, respectively. Property begins with the idea that I have got this, it is mine. Marriage begins with people simply living with each other, and in the case of monogamous marriage, having a sexual monopoly on each other. Why are we not satisfied with these arrangements? Why is it not enough that I possess this in the sense that I have physical control over it and why is it not enough that we just live together? Well, for some people and perhaps for some simple societies it is enough; but many of us think we are better off if there is a system of collectively recognized rights, responsibilities, duties, obligations, and powers added onto—and in the end able to substitute for—brute physical possession and cohabitation. For one thing, we can have a much more stable system of expectations if we add this deontic apparatus; for another, we don't have to rely on brute physical force to sustain the arrangements; and for a third, we can maintain the arrangements even in the absence of the original physical setup. For example, people can remain married even though they have not lived with each other for years, and they can own property even though the property is a long way away from them.

Whatever the advantages and disadvantages, the logically more primitive arrangements have evolved into institutional structures with collectively recognized status-functions. Just as in the case of money, we have imposed, by collective intentionality, new status-functions on things that cannot perform those functions without that collective imposition. However, one special feature of these cases is that often the function is imposed by way of performing explicit speech acts. In such cases the speech act itself is an instance of a status-function imposed on a status-function; and it is used to create new or alter old status-functions. Thus, for example, a marriage ceremony consists in a series of speech acts, but in that context the ceremony creates a new institutional entity, the marriage. The existence of the marriage imposes status-functions on the principals, marked by the terms "husband" and "wife." In order to do that, the speech acts have to have status-functions that go beyond the literal meaning of the words uttered, which is already a status-function.

Let us explore this point in more detail for the case of marriage. The next step in the gradual creation of institutional facts out of more primitive biological phenomena involves the imposition of status-functions, not just on entities that are physically unrelated to the performance of the function but also on entities that have already had a function imposed on them, especially speech acts. And these speech acts are used to impose new status-functions on entities that are not speech acts, for example, on people. Thus in these cases, in the formula "X counts as Y in C," the X element can already be a speech act. Consider, for example, the sort of speech acts people perform in a marriage ceremony. Performing such and such speech acts (the X term) in front of a presiding official (the C term) now counts as getting married (the Y term). Saying those very same words in a different context, while making love, for example, will not constitute getting married. The Y term now assigns a new status to those speech acts. The promises made in the wedding ceremony create a new institutional fact, a marriage, because in that context, making those promises counts as getting married. Furthermore, the whole notion of a "presiding official" specifies a context C that is the result of some previous imposition of function. The whole notion of an official is the notion of an institutional status imposed on some person according to the structure X counts as Y in C. In such a case the presence of the presiding official is the C term in the marriage ceremony, but that he or she is the presiding official is the result of being the Y term in an earlier imposition of status-function.

If we are right in thinking that marriage is typical of many institutions, then it is a consequence of the account that there will be a hierarchical structure of the creation of a large number of institutional facts. Thus, going through the example of marriage: Making certain noises counts as uttering an English sentence, uttering a certain sort of English sentence in certain circumstances counts as making a promise, making a promise in certain circumstances counts as entering into a contract, entering into certain sorts of contracts counts as getting married. The marriage ceremony creates a new institutional fact, the marriage, by imposing a special function on a set of speech acts. But the creation of the marriage imposes a new status and therefore a new function on the individuals involved. They are now "husband" and "wife." And the fact that they are husband and wife, like the marriage itself, is an institutional fact.

I hope it is clear from these examples that a pattern is emerging. The crucial questions to ask are, On what exactly are the status-functions imposed and what exactly are the imposed status-functions? In the case of language and money the answers are relatively simple: for language the statuses are imposed on types of sounds and marks; and though the functions of language are numerous, the primary functions are those of representing the world in the various speech act modes.[1] For money, the statuses have typically been imposed on bits of metal and paper, and the function are those of serving as a medium of exchange, repository of value, etc. In the case of marriage, the situation is a little more complicated. The status is initially imposed on a set of speech acts, those that constitute the marriage ceremony, but those speech acts function to create a new institutional fact, the marriage. But the marriage itself imposes new status-functions on the parties involved, the status-functions of being husband and wife, which carry specific rights and obligations. Now this pattern, the creation of a new institutional fact, usually by the performance of a speech act, where the speech act itself imposes a function on people, buildings, cars, etc., is characteristic of a large number of social institutions. Property, citizenship, licensed drivers, cathedrals, declared wars, and sessions of parliament all exhibit this pattern. The pattern, to put it in a nutshell, is this: We create a new institutional fact, such as a marriage, by using an object (or objects) with an existing status-function, such as a sentence, whose existence is itself an institutional fact, to perform a certain type of speech act, the fact of whose performance is yet another institutional fact.

Let us apply these lessons to the example of property. As usual we need to distinguish between the institution and particular token instances or invocations of that institution, between the general structure "X counts as Y in C" and particular instances of that structure. As I said earlier, property begins in sheer physical possession. In many legal systems, but especially in English common law and those legal systems influenced by it, there is a crucial distinction between real property and personal property. In many countries only the king could own land. Of several crucial distinctions between real and personal property, one which is especially interesting for our investigation is that possession is typically manifested quite differently for real property than for personal property. I can wear my shirt, drive my car, even carry my computer, but when it comes to my house and land, maintenance of my possession requires status indicators. The French distinction between *"meuble"* and *"immeuble"* reveals precisely this distinction. Movable property often also has status indicators—for example, registration papers for cars and brands for cattle. The status indicators in these cases are for such incidental reasons as that the property is very valuable, as in the case of jewelry and oil paintings; or it is not easily identifiable and can wander away, as in the case of cattle; or it carries responsibility for possible harm as in the case of guns; or there are combinations of these reasons, as in the case of cars. In any case, it is hard to see how there could be a system of complex real property ownership without documentation.

On top of the brute physical possession of material objects, including land, we build a structure of buying and selling, of bequeathing, partial transfer, mortgaging, etc., of property. The characteristic devices used are speech acts—deeds, bills of sale, registration papers, wills, etc.; and it is no accident that these are usually called legal "instruments." All are cases of status-functions imposed on speech acts. And, of course, the original speech act is already a case of imposed status-function. So, for example, a bill of sale simply records the fact that I sold you, for example, my car. It is an assertive speech act, but it now can *count as* your title to the car pending the issuance of new registration papers.

Once a society has the institution of property, new property rights are usually created by speech acts, as when I give something to someone, or by speech acts accompanied by other sorts of acts, as when I exchange property for money. Suppose I give my watch to my son. I can do this by saying, "It's yours," "You can have it," or more pompously with the performative, "I hereby give you my watch." I have now imposed a new status-function on these speech acts, that of transferring ownership. These speech acts in turn impose a new status-function on the watch, that of belonging to my son, that of being his property.

I said that the institutional structures enable brute physical possession in the case of property, or brute physical proximity in the case of marriage, to be replaced by a recognized set of relationships whereby people can be married even though they are not living with each other, and people can own property even though the property is far away from them. To achieve this remarkable intellectual feat, we must have what I have called *status indicators.* Just as the paper certificates, when they were redeemable in gold, were status indicators for value, so we have an acknowledged system of legally recognized marriages and property rights. And we have status indicators in the form of marriage certificates, wedding rings, and title deeds, for example. Even when I am a long way from my house or my wife, the institutional structures enable me to remain an owner or a husband, and, if need be, to demonstrate that position to others through the use of status indicators. In such cases, the institutional facts substitute for sheer physical possession and proximity, and the indicators make the institutional facts apparent.

At a more complicated level than money, marriage, and property, governments have their origin in a series of primitive biological phenomena, such as the tendency of most primate social groups to form status hierarchies, the tendency of animals to accept leadership from other animals, and, in some cases, the sheer brute physical force that some animals can exert over others. I do not suggest that this list comprises the whole story of the basis of government, but it seems to me these elements of primate biology are just as essential to understanding political philosophy as many of the features that are traditionally discussed, such as the social contract.

The elaborate structures that are then set up—structures of citizenships, rights, and responsibilities, powers and offices, elections and impeachments, and of other methods of selecting the governors and removing them from office, and all the rest of it—then evolve as institutional structures by way of the collective imposition of status-functions on top of the more primitive relationships.

There is a scale that goes from freedom to necessity, from arbitrariness to reason, in the items selected for the status-functions. At one extreme of freedom and arbitrariness is money. All sorts of substances can serve as money; objects need only meet certain minimum conditions of durability, handleability, transportability, noncounterfeitability, recognizability, and perhaps a few others to perform the functions of money. At the other extreme of necessity and reason are such things as the standard meter rod kept by the French government at the pavillon de Breteuil in Sèvres. By the nature of the case, the sorts of things on which this status-function can be imposed are very restricted. Not just any old object, not even any old meter-long object, can serve this function. In the intermediate range are such X conditions as the promises made in a marriage ceremony or the tests a man had to pass before becoming a knight in the Middle Ages. They are not arbitrarily related to the new functions, of marriage and knighthood, to the degree that paper is arbitrarily related to the function of money; but at the same time they are not matters of necessity either. One can imagine and even construct all sorts of perfectly acceptable ways of getting married or becoming a knight. And because of this slack between the conditions specified by the X term and the function specified by the Y term, cultures differ in the qualifications they require for the performance of the same or similar functions. For example, in most American states, the status of "attorney" requires the possession of a graduate law degree, passing a state bar exam, and swearing in. In Britain, on the other hand, no graduate law degree is required, but such things as being articled to a solicitor for a certain period of time or dining regularly at the Inns of Court count towards qualification. It is not at all obvious how these two different sets of conditions are supposed to enable the possessor to serve the same function, that of legal counsel. Nonetheless, the respective accrediting agencies apparently think they do.

The bifurcation of the imposition of status-functions into the X and Y components has some important consequences for our investigation. First, the status expressions admit of two definitions, one in terms of the constitution (the X term) and one in terms of the imposed agentive function (the Y term). Thus currency can be defined in terms of its origin and structure: Certain sorts of paper issued by the Bureau of Engraving and Printing (X term) are U.S. currency. But currency can also be in part defined as, and indeed is described on the face of U.S. currency as, "legal tender for all debts, public and private" (Y term). A touchdown is when you break the plane of the goal line with the ball in your possession while the play is in progress (X term), and a touchdown is six points (Y term).

Codification

A test for the presence of genuine institutional facts is whether or not we could codify the rules explicitly. In the case of many institutional facts, such as property, marriage, and money, these indeed have been codified into explicit laws. Others, such as friendship, dates, and cocktail parties, are not so codified, but they could be. If people believe that a certain set of relationships in which they are involved is a case of friendship/date/cocktail party, then the possession of each such status is constituted by the belief that the relationship does in fact possess that status, and the possession of the status carries with it certain functions. This is shown by the fact that the people involved have certain sorts of justified expectations from a friendship/date/cocktail party, which they do not have from an identical set of arrangements about which they do not believe that it is a friendship/date/cocktail party. Such institutional patterns could be codified if it mattered tremendously whether or not something was really a cocktail party or only a tea party. If the rights and duties of friendship suddenly became a matter of some grave legal or moral question, then we might imagine these informal institutions becoming codified explicitly, though of course, explicit codification has its price. It deprives us of the flexibility, spontaneity, and informality that the practice has in its uncodified form.

It should be clear from these examples that there is a gradual transition and not a sharp dividing line between social facts in general and the special subclass of institutional facts. In my society "going for a walk with someone" names a social fact but not an institutional fact, because the label assigns no new status-functions. It just labels the intentionality and its manifestation. The characteristic institutional move, however, is that form of collective intentionality that constitutes the acceptance, recognition, etc., of one phenomenon as a phenomenon of a higher sort by imposing a collective status and a corresponding function upon it. The function is always internally related to the status in the sense that it could not be that status if it did not have that function. The criterion is always this: Does the assignment of the label carry with it the assignment of some new functions, for example, in the form of rights and responsibilities, which can be performed only if there is collective acceptance of the function? By this criterion, "husband," "leader," and "teacher" all name status-functions; but "drunk," "nerd," "intellectual," and "celebrity" do not. And, to repeat, it should be obvious that there is no sharp dividing line.

A fascinating test case for this account is war. War is always a form of collective intentionality; hence it is a war only if people think it is a war. But in typical wars, the sheer events count as having a certain legal or quasi-legal status that is supposed to impose certain responsibilities and rights on the participants; and in such cases the war is more than just a social fact; it is an institutional fact. Furthermore, as with marriage, there are ways in which the institutional status is supposed to be imposed. Thus in the case of the war in Korea, the American authorities at the time were very anxious that it not be called "the Korean War" (it was called "the Korean conflict") because it did not satisfy the legal definition of war, since no war had been legally declared in accordance with the Constitutional provision for a declaration of war. They had a choice: If it was a "war," it was unconstitutional; so it was not a "war"; it was a "United Nations police action," a different status-function altogether. Since the phenomenon did not satisfy the X term for imposing the status-function, the Y term "war" was not applied. By the time of the Vietnam War, these sorts of evasions had been abandoned and the sheer physical and intentional facts warranted the application of the term "war," even though the legal situation was no more that of a declared war than had been the case in Korea.

"War" thus oscillates between naming a type of large-scale social fact and a type of institutional fact. The test for the distinction is whether the term "war" is used to label an existing set of relations or whether it implies further consequences that derive from its recognized status as a "war." This is related to how the war came to exist. War as social fact can exist no matter how it came about, but under the U.S. Constitution, war as an institutional fact exists only if it is created by an act of Congress, a type of speech act I call a Declaration. Perhaps after Vietnam and the Persian Gulf

War, we are evolving an institution of common law war, like common law marriage.

Some of the Issues at Stake in the Analysis

In this chapter we address one of the hardest questions of all. What is the logical structure of the creation of institutional facts? Related to that question are the questions, What sorts of facts can we create simply by collective agreement to count an X as having the status Y? And what are the possibilities and limitations of institutional facts? Because the whole system works only by collective acceptance, it would seem a priori that there is not much we could do with it, and it all looks very fragile, as if the whole system might just collapse at any time. Yet the institutional structure of society has precisely this form, so we need to find out its possibilities and limitations.

Because I am trying to describe the logical structure of organized society, it may be well to pause at this point to explain what is involved and to make explicit at least part of what is at stake. How can "organized society" have a "*logical* structure"? After all, society is not a set of propositions or a theory, so what is this talk of logical structure? On my account, social and institutional reality contain representations, not only mental representations but even linguistic representations, as constitutive elements. These do have logical structures. I am attempting to lay bare the most fundamental of those logical structures.

And what is at stake? It is tempting to think that such institutional structures as property and the state itself are maintained by the armed police and military power of the state, and that acceptance will be compelled where necessary. But in the United States, and in several other democratic societies, it is the other way around. The armed might of the state depends on the acceptance of systems of constitutive rules, much more than conversely. This was apparent at the time of the well-televised street riots in Los Angeles in 1992. Looters walked out of stores carrying valuable property while the police pointed their guns at them and ordered them to stop. The looters simply ignored the police, with no further consequences. "Why are you doing this?" asked one reporter. "It's free," the thief replied. All this was watched by millions on television. The police power of the government is usable only against very small numbers, and even then on the assumption that nearly everyone else accepts the systems of status-functions. Once the number of lawbreakers is more than tiny, the police typically retreat to the station house, or put on a ceremonial show of acting as if they were enforcing the law, as in Los Angeles, or quite often arrest the law-abiding citizenry. In Berkeley during the same period of rioting and looting, a store owner was arrested because he had armed himself with the intent of defending his store, and this arrest occurred while looters robbed nearby stores unhindered by the police. In many democratic societies, once the number of lawbreakers reaches critical mass, the police force is largely for show.*

The point for our present discussion is that we cannot assume that the system of acceptance is backed by a credible system of force. For one thing the system of force is itself a system of acceptance. Police forces and armies, for example, are systems of status-functions. But more important for our present purposes, the system of force presupposes the other systems of status-functions. We cannot assume that Leviathan will come to our aid in a genuine crisis; on the contrary, we are in a state of nature all the time, but the state of nature is precisely one in which people do in fact accept systems of constitutive rules, at least nearly all the time.

More spectacular examples are provided by the collapse of the Soviet empire in the *annus mirabilis*, 1989. Anyone who visited the

---

*I originally became aware of this during my first term as an undergraduate at Oxford, when I attended the annual Guy Fawkes riots of that era. The Proctors and Bulldogs apprehended me, a passive spectator, rather than confront the actual participants, who were much too dangerous.

countries of the Soviet empire over the generation prior to 1989 could see that the whole thing was maintained only by a system of terror. Most people did not think that the system of status-functions was morally acceptable, much less socially desirable. But there did not seem to be anything that anyone could do about it because the whole system was maintained by an elaborate apparatus of police powers backed by the armed might of the Soviet military forces. Efforts at reform such as the Czechoslovak "Prague Spring" of 1968 were brutally crushed by the Soviet Army with the help of the domestic secret police. In Czechoslovakia, every tenth person was made to spy on the other nine and report any sign of disaffection to the secret political police. In the GDR the system of police surveillance was even more thorough and ruthless, to the point that even husbands and wives were forced to report on each other. No one—no qualified expert on the Soviet system, no diplomat, no journalist, and no tourist—could predict in the mid-1980s that the whole system would collapse suddenly and within a few years. It collapsed when the system of status-functions was no longer accepted. The fear of Soviet intervention was no longer credible, and the indigenous police and military were unwilling to attempt to maintain the system. In the GDR the army refused to fire on the opposition even when ordered to do so.

I do not believe there is any single motivation for the continued acknowledgment of institutional facts. It is tempting to some to think that there must be some rational basis for such acknowledgment, that the participants derive some game theoretical advantage or get on a higher indifference curve, or some such, but the remarkable feature of institutional structures is that people continue to acknowledge and cooperate in many of them even when it is by no means obviously to their advantage to do so. When institutions are maintained largely by habit, they can also collapse quite suddenly, as when people lose confidence in their currency or cease to recognize their government as a government.

Marx, believing that the most fundamental interests were class interests, said that all history is the history of class struggle. But the surprising thing is how little of history is about class struggles. In the great upheavals of the twentieth century, for example, national loyalties proved much more powerful than class solidarity, and conationals of all classes slaughtered enemy nationals of all classes with passion and enthusiasm. International class solidarity counted for next to nothing. And in most of these great upheavals, the systems of constitutive rules that sustained the class distinctions were preserved, even though all sorts of other institutional changes took place; and in places where the institutional structures sustaining the class structure were destroyed—for example, Russia in the first war, China after the second—their destruction was not one of the war aims of their enemies. Imperial Germany was not out to create a Bolshevik state in Russia, nor was Maoism an objective of the Greater East Asia Coprosperity Sphere. The point I am trying to illustrate is that there is no simple set of relations among motivation, self-interest, institutional structure, and institutional change.

Perhaps the most amazing form of status-function is in the creation of *human* rights. Prior to the European Enlightenment the concept of rights had application only within some institutional structure—property rights, marital rights, droit de seigneur, etc. But somehow the idea came to be collectively accepted that one might have a status-function solely by virtue of being a human being, that the X term was "human" and the Y term was "possessor of inalienable rights." It is no accident that the collective acceptance of this move was aided by the idea of divine authority: "they are endowed by their Creator with certain unalienable rights, that among these are Life, Liberty and the pursuit of Happiness." The idea of human rights has survived the decline of religious belief, and has even become internationalized. The Helsinki Declaration on Human Rights is frequently appealed to, with varying degrees of effectiveness, against dictatorial regimes. Lately there has even been a movement for the recognition of animal rights. Both human and animal rights are cases of the imposition of status-function through collective intentionality.

In general status-functions are matters of power, as we will see in the rest of this chapter. The structure of institutional facts is a structure of power relations, including negative and positive, conditional and categorical, collective and individual powers. In our intellectual tradition since the Enlightenment the whole idea of power makes a certain type of liberal sensibility very nervous. A certain class of intellectuals would rather that power did not exist at all (or if it has to exist they would rather that their favorite oppressed minority had lots more of it and everyone else had lots less). One lesson to be derived from the study of institutional facts is this: everything we value in civilization requires the creation and maintenance of institutional power relations through collectively imposed status-functions. These require constant monitoring and adjusting to create and preserve fairness, efficiency, flexibility, and creativity, not to mention such traditional values as justice, liberty, and dignity. But institutional power relations are ubiquitous and essential. Institutional power—massive, pervasive, and typically invisible—permeates every nook and cranny of our social lives, and as such it is not a threat to liberal values but rather the precondition of their existence.

Some Types of Imposition of Status-Functions

In order to investigate the logical structure of institutional reality, I first want to ask: what *sorts* of new facts, new powers, new causal structures can people create by creating status-functions, when status-functions exist only because they are believed to exist?

Where physical functions are concerned the only limitations are provided by the sheer physical possibilities. The history of technology is the history of how accumulated knowledge and organized desires have utilized technical possibilities. But when it comes to institutional facts, improvements in technology do not change the possibilities. We cannot impose an electrical charge just by deciding to count something as an electrical charge, but we can impose the office of the Presidency just by deciding what we will count as becoming President, and then making those people President who meet the conditions we have decided on. The intensionality-with-an-s of the sentence form "X counts as Y in C" is a clue to the intentionality-with-a-t of the phenomena. Because neither the X term nor the Y term permits substitution of coreferring expressions without loss or change of truth value of the whole statement, we have good reasons to suppose that the "counts as" locution specifies a form of intentionality. The possibilities of creating institutional facts by the use of this formula are limited by the possibilities of imposing new features on entities just by collectively agreeing that they have those features. Our question now is, What are the forms and limits of the institutional imposition of function?

At first sight institutional facts seem utterly bewildering in their variety. We can make promises, score touchdowns, get tenure, become President, adjourn the meeting, pay our bills, and fire our employees all by way of institutional facts. But within this enormous variety of subject matter there are actually only a very few general formal properties of institutional facts.

Because the creation of institutional facts is a matter of imposing a status and with it a function on some entity that does not already have that status-function, in general the creation of a status-function is a matter of conferring some new *power*. There would not be much point to imposing the status-function named by the Y term if it did not confer some new power on the X term, and most (not all) creations of institutional facts are precisely conferring powers on the X term, or performing some truth functional operation such as negation and conditionalization on the creation of the power. In the simplest case, the Y term names a power that the X term does not have solely in virtue of its X structure. In cases where the X term is a person, that person acquires powers that he or she did not already have. In cases where the X term is an object, the user of that object can do things with it that he or she could not do solely in virtue of its X structure. Thus money, passports, driver's licenses, and sentences of a language enable the bearer or user to do things he or she could not otherwise do, such as buy things, travel between countries, drive a car legally, and perform speech acts by uttering the sentences. In these cases the acceptance of the Y status involves some form of creation of power such as authorization, permission, enablement. Other cases, as we will see, involve some Boolean function on these forms of power such as negation or conditionalization.

So the question How many types of institutional facts could there be? boils down in large part to the question What sorts of power can we create just by collective agreement? Sheer physical power is unaffected by collective agreement. We can't add to our weight or arm-wrestling abilities by collective agreement. But we can and do increase people's wealth, or even give them the power of life and death over us, by collective agreement. The general form of the answer must be: We can with this mechanism create all and only those forms of power where the collective recognition or acceptance of the power is *constitutive* of having it. If this is the formal structure of the mechanism, then two puzzling features are automatically accounted for. First, the mechanism places no restrictions on subject matter so the enormous variety of institutional reality, from wives to warfare, and from cocktail parties to Congress, should seem less puzzling. Second, the mechanism so described does not require that the participants be aware of what is actually happening. They may think that the man is King only because he is divinely anointed, but as long as they continue to recognize his authority, he has the status-function of king, regardless of whatever false beliefs they may hold.

There is an interesting class of exceptions to the claim that all institutional facts involve power. Some institutional facts involve pure status with no further function. These are the cases where the status is purely honorific. If you are awarded a medal, given an honorary degree, voted the most popular person in your class, or become Miss Alameda County, there are in general no rights or powers associated with these positions. They are purely honorific.

Their opposites are matters of negative honors. Thus, if you are censured for your bad behavior, reprimanded by your superiors, or voted the least popular in your class, these are all negative honors. No further powers, positive or negative, need apply.

Our question is, In the formula "X counts as Y in C," how many types of "Y"s are there? Because institutional facts are structured by collective intentionality and because there are strict limitations on the possibilities of creating institutional facts, we ought to be able to answer this question. So let us begin naively by listing some formal features of institutional reality.

The Y status can be imposed on several different ontological categories of phemomena: People (e.g., chairmen, wives, priests, professors); objects (e.g., sentences, five dollar bills, birth certificates, driver's licenses); and events (elections, weddings, cocktail parties, wars, touchdowns). The people, objects, and events interact in systematic relationships (e.g., governments, marriages, corporations, universities, armies, churches). Often the Y status is imposed on people and groups of people in virtue of a set of preexisting preinstitutional relations among them. Thus a collection of people might constitute a city-state, or a man and woman might constitute a married couple, but such constitution is not simply in virtue of being a collection of people of the right size, but rather in virtue of the relations among the members of the collection.

What then are the features of objects, events, and people that are imposed by the new status-functions? My first suggestion is that the category of people, including groups, is fundamental in the sense that the imposition of status-functions on objects and events works only in relation to people. This should not be surprising, since it is a general feature of agentive functions. It is not the five dollar bill as an *object* that matters, but rather that the *possessor* of the five dollar bill now has a certain power that he or she did not otherwise have. Just so, it is not the screwdriver as an object that matters, but rather that the possessor of the screwdriver now has a power that he or she did not otherwise have.

This suggests what I think is in fact the case, that the content of the collective intentionality in the imposition of the status-function will typically be that some human subject, singular or plural, has some power, positive or negative, conditional or categorical. This will be directly the case where the status is imposed on an agent, as in, e.g., Jones is President, and indirectly the case where the status is imposed on an object, as in, e.g., this is a five dollar bill.

Another formal feature to note is that the usual distinction between the internal and the external points of view applies to institutional facts. In this book we are interested primarily in the internal point of view, because it is only from the internal point of view of the participants that the institution can exist at all. The anthropologist from outside the institution may see the potlatch, for example, as performing functions of which the Kwakiutl participants are totally unaware, but the whole feast is a potlatch in the first place only because of the collective intentionality and the imposition of status-functions by the participants, and this, whether conscious or unconscious, can exist only from the internal first-person point of view.

Even within the internal point of view there are some formal distinctions to be made. At the microlevel the individual sees money as a medium of exchange and store of value and he or she sees marriage as a collective lifetime promise between a male and a female partner. But at a macrolevel, planners and organizers, even from an internal point of view, see the institutions as having different functions, though the status assigned in individual cases is the same. The bishop sees the function of marriage as glorifying God and producing social stability, and the central bank sees the supply of money as a way of controlling the economy. The important point is that the internal microlevel is ontologically primary. There is no way that the bishop, the head of the Federal Reserve Board, and the anthropologist can have their points of view without the lowest-level participants in the very trenches of money and marriage having the basic form of intentionality that constitutes the structure of institutional facts. Furthermore, the microlevel participants may have all sorts of other functions that they want the institutional entities to perform for them that are irrelevant to the basic ontology. Thus many people want money for power and prestige, and for them that is a basic function of money. Among the ruling dynasties of Europe marriage was a tool of dynastic power. (*Alii bella gerunt, tu felix Austria nube:* Happy Austria, other nations wage wars, you marry.) And marriage has performed such ulterior functions even among the humble. The point is that all this works only given the basic ontology of the ordinary collective intentionality in the street, so to speak, imposing a status-function according to the formula.

If we look at institutional facts with these points in mind, it seems to me that status-functions fall into certain broad categories. As a first stab at classifying these—we will have to make improvements later—I will provisionally divide them into four broad categories, which I call Symbolic, Deontic, Honorific, and Procedural.

1.   Symbolic Powers: The Creation of Meaning

The point of having symbolic powers is to enable us to represent reality in one or more of the possible illocutionary modes. In such cases we impose intentionality on entities that are not intrinsically intentional. And to do this is to create language and meaning in all its forms. The imposition of the intentionality on a certain type of physical structure determines both a formal structure—the *syntax*—and a meaningful content—the *semantics*. Thus, for example, the phonetic/graphemic type *"Il pleut"* counts as a sentence of French, and *"Es regnet"* counts as a sentence of German. On physical sounds and marks we impose the statuses word, sentence, and syntax generally. And on different syntactical objects we have in these cases imposed the same semantic content. They both mean "it's raining." Symbolization is essential to the other forms of the imposition of institutional function. For reasons I tried to explain in Chapter 3, we cannot impose rights, obligations, etc., without words or symbols.

2.   *Deontic Powers: The Creation of Rights and Obligations*

The point of having deontic powers is to regulate relations between people. In this category, we impose rights, responsibilities, obligations, duties, privileges, entitlements, penalties, authorizations, permissions, and other such deontic phenomena. On our earlier suggestion, that in general the Y status confers (or denies) power, the obvious hypothesis would be that there are two broad categories of such status-functions. The first is where the agent is endowed with some new power, certification, authorization, entitlement, right, permission, or qualification granting the ability to do something he or she could not otherwise have done; and the second is where the agent is required, obligated, in duty bound, penalized, enjoined, or otherwise compelled to do something he or she would not otherwise have had to do—or, what amounts to the same thing, prevented from doing something that would otherwise have been doable. Roughly speaking, the two major categories are those of positive and negative powers. To have a label, let us say that all deontic status-functions are matters of *conventional power*. This terminology enables us to distinguish conventional power from brute physical power, even though of course the two often go hand in hand; because often the point of giving conventional power is to authorize the use of brute physical power. Police power is an obvious example.

If we take as our primary target of analysis not the social objects, such as money, governments, and universities, but the agents who operate on and within those objects, then the great divide in the categorization of institutional reality is between what the agent *can* do and what the agent *must* (and must not) do, between what the agent is *enabled* to do and what he or she is *re-*

quired to do as a result of the assignment of status specified in the Y term. Here are some examples:

John has one thousand dollars in the bank.
Tom is a citizen of the United States.
Clinton is President.
Sally is an attorney.
Sam owns a restaurant.

Each of these assigns rights and responsibilities. The first example assigns to John the right to buy things or employ people with his money and the duty to pay taxes on interest earned by the money. The second example assigns to Tom the right, among many others, to vote in elections and the obligation, among many others, of getting a Social Security number. The third example assigns to Clinton the right to veto legislation and the responsibility of delivering a State of the Union address to Congress, etc. Notice also that institutional facts that assign rights and responsibilities can also be destroyed or eliminated in various ways. Here are some examples:

Ann lost all her money.
Ivan's fortune in rubles has become worthless through inflation.
Nixon resigned from office.
Coolidge's term expired.
Sam got divorced.
Sally's husband died.

3. *Honor: Status for Its Own Sake*

The point of honors (and dishonors) is to have statuses valued (or disvalued) for their own sake, rather than just for their further consequences. Examples are victory and defeat in games, and institutionally sanctioned forms of public honor and disgrace. Here are some examples:

Mark won the Far West skiing championship.
McCarthy was censured by the U.S. Senate.
Bill was awarded a medal by the Collège de France.

In addition to these three categorical types of status-functions, we need also to identify the conditional or procedural features of deontic powers and honors.

4.   *Procedural Steps on the Way to Power and Honor*

Within institutions we can assign procedural stages toward the achievement of either rights and responsibilities or honors and disgraces. Here are some examples:

Bill voted for Reagan.
Clinton was nominated the Democratic candidate for President.
The objection was sustained by the judge.

In the case of voting, though one has a right to vote, the actual casting of the vote does not create any new rights and responsibilities by itself. Only the accumulated set of votes establishes a winner with the requisite majority and therefore with new rights and responsibilities. Getting six votes is like getting six points in a football game, but unlike getting six dollars. Six votes and six points are procedural steps on the way to winning, but you can't do anything else with them. With six dollars you can actually buy something. Again, when a candidate is nominated for the Presidency, he or she does acquire new rights and responsibilities as a candidate, but the whole point of the candidacy is supposed to be that it is a stage on the way to becoming President.

———

One and the same institutional fact can involve all four of the preceding features. Thus becoming a Democratic nominee gives the person so nominated certain rights and responsibilities, it is a great honor, and it is a procedural stage on the road to becoming President, and the whole thing could not exist without words or other sorts of symbols, as I explained in Chapter 3.

I want to illustrate these points by showing how they apply to the case of games. Games are especially useful objects of study for this analysis because they provide a microcosm of larger social phenomena. Famously, Wittgenstein argued that there is no essence marked by the word "game." But all the same, there are certain common features possessed by paradigmatic games such as those in competitive sports—baseball, football, tennis, etc. In each case the game consists of a series of attempts to overcome certain obstacles that have been created for the purpose of trying to overcome them. Each side in the game tries to overcome the obstacles and prevent the other side from overcoming them.* The rules of the game specify what the obstacles are and what can be done to overcome them, as well as what must and what must not be done. Thus in baseball the rules allow the batter to swing at the ball, but they do not require him to swing. However, after he gets three strikes he must leave the batter's box and let someone else bat. Most of the rules of the game have to do with rights and obligations (feature 2) but the overall aim is winning (feature 3) and many of the intervening steps are procedural (feature 4). For example, several of the rights and obligations are conditional. Thus if a batter has one strike or three balls, that does not so far give him any further rights or obligations, but it establishes conditional rights and obligations: two more strikes and he is out, one more ball and he is walked to first base. Such conditional rights and obligations are typical of institutional structures. For example, in American universities, after so many years of service you are entitled to be considered for a tenure position.

---

*This answer to Wittgenstein on games was not invented by me. I do not know who first thought of it or where I first heard it, but it has become part of the oral tradition.

The Logical Structure of Conventional Power

To further explore the issues raised in the tentative taxonomy of the previous section, I now want to examine the intentional structure of institutional facts. My aim is to try to state the general form of the content of the Y status-function when we go from X to Y in the formula "X counts as Y in C." Because the Y content is imposed on the X element by collective acceptance, there must be some content to these collective acceptances (recognitions, beliefs, etc.); and I am suggesting that for a large class of cases the content involves some conventional power mode in which the subject is related to some type of action or course of actions. Furthermore, because there are strict limits on what sorts of powers can be created by collective acceptance, we ought to be able to state the general forms of the content of the Y term in a very small number of formulae. Because power is always the power to do something or constrain someone else from doing something, the propositional content of power status-functions is always in part that

(S does A)

where "S" is to be replaced by an expression referring either to a single individual or a group, and "A" by the name of an act, action, or activity, including negatives such as refraining or abstaining.

Following this line of thought, we see that the primitive structure of the collective intentionality imposed on the X term, where X counts as Y in C, is

We accept (S has power (S does A)).

Formally speaking, one can perform a number of operations on this basic structure, and these operations exemplify several distinctions I have made. As mentioned earlier, there is a distinction between positive and negative conventional powers, the distinction between *enablements* and *requirements*. There is also a distinction between the *creation* and *destruction* of conventional powers. Examples of this are the distinctions between marriage

and divorce, and between appointing someone to an office and removing him or her from office. There is moreorver a distinction
between *procedural* and *terminal* conventional powers. An example of this is the distinction between receiving a certain number of
votes and winning the election. Getting votes is a procedural step
on the way to winning, and winning is the terminus of the elec-
toral process. There is also the distinction between the initial creation and the subsequent maintenance of an institutional fact. I
will discuss this distinction in the next chapter.

Let us begin our investigation of these formal operations by ex-
ploring the two basic modes of enablement and requirement,
which can be represented as

> We accept (S is enabled (S does A)).
> We accept (S is required (S does A)).

In the case of enablements we collectively grant power to some individual or group; in the case of requirements we collectively re-
strict the power of some individual or group.

On the hypothesis that I am pursuing, if we put all these elements together, the underlying form of a typical enabling conventional power, e.g., "X, this piece of paper, counts as Y, a five dollar
bill," would be in part

> We accept (S, the bearer of X, is enabled (S buys with X up to
> the value of five dollars)).*

And in the case of negative conventional powers, i.e., requirements, for example, "X, this piece of paper, counts as Y, a parking
ticket," the underlying form of the collective intentionality would
be in part

---

*And remember, don't be worried by the apparent circularity of using institu-
tional notions such as "buy" or "value of five dollars" in the account of the intentional content, since these notions cash out in ways I tried to explain in Chapter
2; that is, they cash out not by our eliminating the circle but by widening it.

We accept (S, the person to whom X is issued, is required
        (S pays a fine within a specified period)).

So far we have described the form of ongoing institutional facts, where, for example, we already have a five dollar bill or a parking ticket. But these conventional powers are themselves created or destroyed. And these acts of creation and destruction may be exercises of conventional power, for example, marriage and divorce; or they may simply grow, as, for example, a group may gradually come to accept someone as its leader without a formal election or appointment. In cases where the act is one of explicit creation or destruction of a conventional power, it is itself typically the exercise of another conventional power, the power to so create or destroy. Suppose a conventional power-creating agency, such as the Department of Motor Vehicles, issues a driver's license to an applicant S. What is the form of the collective intentionality? We need to distinguish the intentionality of the agency from that of the surrounding society, which makes the whole system work in the first place. From the point of view of the surrounding society, the form of the creation of the institutional power is

We accept (The agency creates (S is enabled (S drives a car))).

When a conventional power is destroyed, it seems to me the negation operates on the collective acceptance and not on the content of that acceptance. Thus, for example, if the marriage between S1 and S2 is dissolved, the consequence is that

We no longer accept (S1 and S2 are married to each other).

It is tempting to think that one ought to be able to define all conventional powers in terms of one primitive plus negation. The successes we have had in other branches of logic encourage this temptation. Thus in alethic modal logic

$$\Box(p) \text{ iff} \sim \Diamond(\sim p)$$

(It is necessarily the case that p if and only if it is not possibly the case that not p)

And in quantificational logic:

$$\forall x(fx) \text{ iff} \sim \exists x(\sim fx)$$

(For every objeĭct x, x has feature f if and only if there is no object x such that x does not have f)

And even in some systems of deontic logic:

$$O(p) \text{ iff} \sim P(\sim p)$$

(It is obligatory that p if and only if it is not permissible that not p.)

So why not a parallel structure in "institutional" logic? Why not

S is enabled (S does A) iff~S is required (~S does A).?

(S is enabled to perform act A if and only if it is not the case that S is required not to perform act A.)

At first sight the parallelism would not seem to work because the absence of a requirement not to do something does not by itself constitute an institutional enablement to do it. In classic deontic logic the absence of the obligatoriness not to do something is equivalent to the permissibility of doing it; but there is no such obvious equivalence for conventional powers, because there are lots of things that I am not required not do to (i.e., they are not forbidden), but I have not been institutionally authorized or enabled to do them. For example, I have not been institutionally enabled to get up and walk around the room, blow my nose, or scratch my head, even though it is not the case that I have been required not to do these things.

However, if we think deeply enough about these issues, we can see that the parallelism holds perfectly. The problem is one of scope. Conventional power exists only where there is some act or process of creation, so we have to think of both institutional enablements and requirements as inside the scope of the collective power creation operator. The way to understand the above biconditional is to understand each clause as inside the scope of the power creation operator, and so understood the parallelism between the law of interchange for modal, deontic, and quantificational logic works perfectly for institutional logic. Thus,

S is enabled (S does A) iff~S is required (~S does A).

really means

We make it the case by collective acceptance that (S is enabled (S does A)) iff we make it the case by collective acceptance that (~ S is required (~ S does A)).

Examples will illustrate the point. When we make it the case that *among the President's powers* the President has the power to veto congressional legislation, we make it the case the *among the President's powers* he is not required not to veto such legislation. Similarly, when I am issued a driver's license, an authorization to drive, I acquire a status such that I am not required not to drive.

There is a deep point implicit in this about the nature of conventional powers: They exist only where there is some act or process of creation. So the mere absence of a conventional power, marked by negation, is not equivalent to the presence of some other sort of conventional power, but we can still define both modes of conventional power in terms of one power plus negation, provided that both are understood as creations according to the formula. The two basic modes of conventional power are those where we impose authorization on an agent and those where we impose a requirement on an agent, and these can be defined in terms of each other plus negation.

Furthermore, we can define destroying a power in terms of removing a previously existing conventional power. For example, when an employee is fired or a court grants a divorce, in each case a previously existing conventional power is destroyed by removing its acceptance. Thus "You're fired!" is equivalent to the removal of conventional power:

We remove the powers (you are employed)

and that is equivalent to

We no longer accept (S has the rights and obligations (S acts as an employee)).

The basic argument for regarding the logical structure of the destruction of conventional power as negations of collective acceptance rather than negations of the content of the acceptance is that they do not require continued maintenance of status-function in a way that conventional power typically does require such maintenance. Thus marriage requires continuous maintenance in a way that divorce does not.

Now, in light of this discussion of the logical structure of institutional reality, where are we left with our preliminary classification of institutional facts into symbolic, deontic, honorific, and procedural? I think it shows that the classification cannot stand as a well-motivated taxonomy because, roughly speaking, everything turns out to be deontic. Consider the procedural cases first. All the examples I gave were cases of steps in iterated deontic and honorific status-functions. Thus, for example, making an X on a ballot paper counts as voting for a candidate, and getting a majority of the votes counts as winning the election. Swinging at the ball and missing counts as a strike, and getting three strikes counts as striking out. In these cases the procedural status-functions are conditional deontic functions, and when the antecedent of the conditional is fulfilled, the result is an upward step in the iterated hierarchy of institutional reality. Thus, for example, having one strike is a conditional deontic status. Its force is that if you get two more you are out. But when you do get two more strikes then you are out, which is a new deontic status, and thus a move upward in the hierarchy of institutional facts. But if the procedural status-functions reduce to conditional deontic and honorific status-functions and can be explained in terms of the iteration of status-function hierarchies, then there is no separate class of procedural status-functions.

Well, what about the honorific cases? It is best to think of them as limiting cases of the deontic. A status valued for its own sake, and not for the power attaching to it, is a limiting case of a status-function. The honorific cases are, in a sense, degenerate cases of the deontic, because the rights and obligations that typically go with the status-functions have shrunk to the point that the status is valued or disvalued only for its own sake. The question, Are the honorific cases really deontic? is like the questions, Is zero really a number? or, Is the null class really a class? The question asks not for a matter of fact but for a decision, and I am suggesting that the most useful decision is not to treat the honorific as a separate category.

The symbolic is also implicitly a special case of the deontic, because the creation of conventional meanings of sentences creates the power in speakers to perform speech acts with those sentences. So in the end we do not have four independent categories. But if it now turns out that everything is a deontic status-function, then the term "deontic" is no longer appropriate because it was designed to express a contrast that can no longer be maintained. The upshot is that from the point of view of logical structure, we cannot maintain the categories of Symbolic, Deontic, Honorific, and Procedural. We simply have creations and destructions of conventional powers. Some of these powers are symbolic, some are purely honorific, some are negative, and some are conditional. Moreover, some are collective and some are individual, some are imposed at the ground floor on brute phenomena, others are imposed on entities that already have conventional powers. As far as subject matter is concerned, we are left with two broad categories of the linguistic, narrowly construed in terms of actual sentences and speech acts, and the nonlinguistic, which includes money, property, marriage, and everything else in institutional reality.

Conclusion

Our discussion of the logical structure of institutional reality supports the following hypothesis. I do not know if it is true and I certainly have not demonstrated it, but it is worth further exploration, and it accounts for the data we have considered so far:

There is exactly one primitive logical operation by which institutional reality is created and constituted. It has this form:

> We collectively accept, acknowledge, recognize, go along
> with, etc., that (S has power (S does A)).

We can abbreviate this formula as

> We accept (S has power (S does A)).

Let us call this "the basic structure." Other cases of status-functions are cases where Boolean operations are performed on the basic structure, or cases where the structure emerges as part of a system of such iterated structures, or cases where the "power" assigned by the structure is purely honorific. Thus, for example, the requirement that I pay my taxes is defined in terms of negation on the basic structure.

> We accept (S is required (S pays taxes)) iff We accept (~S has power (~S pays taxes)).

Having one strike on a batter in a baseball game is a matter of conditionalization and iteration on the basic structure.

> We accept (S has one strike) iff We accept (if S has two more strikes S is out).

And satisfying the antecedent of the conditional automatically raises the structure to a higher level of iterated status-functions, where conventional power becomes manifest.

> We accept (S is out) iff We accept (S is required (S leaves the field)).

And the right-hand side reduces to the basic structure plus negation,

> We accept (~S has power (~S leaves the field)).

I am of course oversimplifying enormously in order to make the underlying logical structure visible. There are lots of other features involved in being out in a baseball game besides just having to leave the field. For example, three outs and the whole side is out. But the idea I am trying to get across is that in the end all these features cash out in terms of conventional powers, and conventional powers are variations on and iterations of the basic structure. I believe that our investigation of the logical features of the intentional content of the Y status-function, in the formula X counts as Y, has begun to show that the enormous complexity of the body of institutional reality has a rather simple skeletal structure. This is not surprising, given the rudimentary apparatus we have to work with. We have nothing but the ability to impose a status, and with it a function, by collective agreement or acceptance. But I do not wish to give the impression that I think I have got to the bottom of these issues. Even if I am right so far, this discussion is only a beginning.

5

The General Theory
of Institutional Facts

Part II: Creation, Maintenance, and the Hierarchy

The Creation and Maintenance of
Institutional Facts

In Chapter 4 we explored the logical structure of institutional facts. With this account of structure in hand, we now have enough material to state a general theory of the creation, maintenance, and identification of institutional facts. In the statement of the general theory I will summarize some of the material of earlier chapters in order to extend it. In this account we need to distinguish four elements: the institution, its use in the creation of facts, their continued existence, and their indication.

First, there is the *institution* that permits the creation of institutional facts out of social facts and brute facts. Such institutions always consist in constitutive rules (practices, procedures) that have the form X counts as Y in context C. There is nothing magical about this formula, and I do not wish to make a fetish of it. The point is that collective intentionality imposes a special status on some phenomenon, and with that status, a function; and I need a formula for representing the structure of that imposition. The Y term imposes a new status on the phenomenon named by the X term, and the new status carries with it a function that cannot be performed just by virtue of the intrinsic physical features named by the X term. The function requires the status in order that it be performed and the status requires collective intentionality, including a continued acceptance of the status with its corresponding function. Typically the associated function is definitionally implicit in the expression that names the status. Thus, for example, the status described by "money" already implies the function of being a medium of exchange, among others. Sometimes the function in question is only very generally specified or implied by the status expression, and sometimes a whole range of functions, rather than a single specific function, may be implied. Thus, for example, the statuses of being a husband or a citizen have associated with them a whole range of functions, and different societies may differ radically in the rights and obligations of husbandhood or citizenship. Nonetheless, even in these cases there is a functional implication carried by the description of the object as having a certain institutional status, as is shown by the fact that categories of assessment are appropriate under the status description that would not otherwise be appropriate. To be a husband or a citizen is already to have the possibility of being a "good" or "bad" husband or citizen.

It is perhaps worth pointing out that by using the notion of function I certainly do not intend to endorse any sort of "functional analysis" or "functional explanations" in sociological investigation. The functions I am discussing are internally related to the corresponding status, and thus in general the statement of the status trivially implies the corresponding function. To say that something is money implies, by definition, that among other things, it functions as a medium of exchange, i.e., as money.

Within the institution we need to distinguish three elements: The initial *creation* of an institutional fact, its continued *existence*, and its official (usually linguistic) *representation* in the form of status indicators.

Typical events that create ongoing institutional facts are property sales, elections, marriage ceremonies, declarations of war, and openings of parliaments, as well as passing laws and adopting constitutions. These often, though not always, involve explicit performative declarations, as, for example, "I declare the parliament in session," "War is hereby declared," "I pronounce you husband and wife." The ongoing existence of institutional facts is described in sentences such as "This is my wife," "Parliament is in session," "There is a war on," "I own that property," and "I am a graduate of Oxford University." Typical examples of official linguistic representations of institutional facts are marriage licenses, title deeds, university diplomas, official uniforms, medals, and driver's licenses.

Let us consider each of these in turn.

The Creation of Institutional Facts

The simplest cases of the creation of institutional facts are those where the institutional structures already guarantee that certain lower-level actions count as higher-level institutional phenomena. Obvious examples are games and speech acts. Making a certain movement of a piece of wood counts as moving the knight to bishop 5 in a game of chess. In a particular context it may also count as putting your king in check. In appropriate circumstances, intentionally saying "I promise to come to see you" counts as promising to come to see you. Crossing the goal line in possession of the ball while a play is in progress counts as scoring a touchdown. And so on for a large number of cases. The complex cases require that certain types of institutional facts be created by acts whose performances are themselves institutional facts. Thus the creation of new property rights typically requires the act of buying/selling or an act of giving, for example. In all these cases new status-functions are imposed on phenomena that already have had status-functions imposed on them. A special case of this type of creation of institutional fact is the use of explicit performative utterances. In such cases a new status-function is imposed on a speech act, the function of imposing a status-function. Thus when the chairman of the parliament says, "I hereby declare the parliament in session," a new status-function is imposed on the speech act, the status-function of making it the case that the parliament is in session. But as a result, the actual assemblage of people now has a status-function imposed on it, that of being a parliament in session, and as such has the power of passing laws.

In principle, there does not appear to be an upper limit to this type of iteration of imposed status-function on imposed status-function. Thus in an election the individual expressions of preference of the voters count as voting in an election. A sequence of such speech acts, when certified by the authorities, counts as an election. Getting a sufficient number of votes counts as winning. Winning and being sworn in count as becoming mayor of a city.

One general principle is this: To the extent that the new institutional status is of major importance, we are more inclined to require that it be created by explicit speech acts performed according to strict rules. And these speech acts are themselves institutional facts. Thus a war is on because it was *declared,* we are husband and wife because we *got married,* Clinton is president because he was elected and has been *sworn in.* Some institutional facts that typically require speech acts for their creation may also come to exist without any speech act, simply by a social fact persisting over a period of time. Thus if there are laws that so provide, a "common law marriage" may come to exist without a marriage ceremony, and property rights may be transferred by "adverse possession" without any sale or gift.

The Continued Existence of Institutional Facts

The secret of understanding the continued existence of institutional facts is simply that the individuals directly involved and a sufficient number of members of the relevant community must continue to recognize and accept the existence of such facts. Because the status is constituted by its collective acceptance, and because the function, in order to be performed, requires the status, it is essential to the functioning that there be continued acceptance of the status. The moment, for example, that all or most of the members of a society refuse to acknowledge property rights, as in a revolution or other upheaval, property rights cease to exist in that society.

One of the most fascinating—and terrifying—features of the era in which I write this is the steady erosion of acceptance of large institutional structures around the world. The breakdown of national identification in favor of ethnic tribalism occurs in places as various as Bosnia, Canada, the former Czechoslovakia, Turkey, and many American universities. In several African countries there is no way to tell where the army ends and the armed bands begin or who is a "military leader" and who a "warlord." In Russia the instability is such that anything one might say with confidence now—about the relations among the state, the military, the secret police, and organized crime, for example—is likely to be out of date by the time you read this. The temptation in all these cases is to think that in the end it all depends on who has the most armed might, that brute facts will always prevail over institutional facts. But that is not really true. The guns are ineffectual except to those who are prepared to use them in cooperation with others and in structures, however informal, with recognized lines of authority and command. And all of that requires collective intentionality and institutional facts.

One of the great illusions of the era is that "Power grows out of the barrel of a gun." In fact power grows out of organizations, i.e., systematic arrangements of status-functions. And in such organizations the unfortunate person with a gun is likely to be among the least powerful and the most exposed to danger. The real power resides with the person who sits at a desk and makes noises through his or her mouth and marks on paper. Such people typically have no weapons other than, at most, a ceremonial pistol and a sword for dress occasions.

Because institutions survive on acceptance, in many cases an elaborate apparatus of prestige and honor is invoked to secure recognition and maintain acceptance. Charles de Gaulle's behavior regarding France, both during and after World War II, was a continuous illustration of these points. By constantly insisting on the honor and prestige of France, by pretending that an independent French government continued to exist during the war, and by constantly insisting that other national leaders acknowledge him as an equal, de Gaulle helped to re-create and maintain the French nation-state. And the point is completely general. Where the institution demands more of its participants than it can extract by force, where consent is essential, a great deal of pomp, ceremony, and razzmatazz is used in such a way as to suggest that something more is going on than simply acceptance of the formula X counts as Y in C. Armies, courtrooms, and to a lesser extent universities employ ceremonies, insignia, robes, honors, ranks, and even music to encourage continued acceptance of the structure. Jails find these devices less necessary because they have brute force.

One way to create institutional facts in situations where the institution does not exist is simply to act as if it did exist. The classic case is the Declaration of Independence in 1776. There was no institutional structure of the form X counts as Y in C, whereby a group of the King's subjects in a British Crown Colony could create their independence by a performative speech act. But the Founding Fathers acted as if their meeting in Philadelphia was a context C such that by performing a certain declarative speech act X they created an institutional fact of independence Y. They got away with this, that is, they created and sustained acceptance of the institutional fact because of local community support and military force, culminating in Cornwallis's surrender at Yorktown.

The formula "X counts as Y" applies to both the creation and the continued existence of the phenomenon, because the constitutive rule is a device for creating the facts, and in general, the existence of the fact is constituted by its having been created and not yet destroyed. Thus going through the ceremony counts as *getting married,* and getting married and not subsequently dying, getting divorced, or having the marriage annulled counts as *being married.* Saying "I declare the parliament open" counts as *opening the parliament,* and for the parliament to have been opened and not subsequently closed counts as its *being in session.*

Status Indicators

Since institutional facts exist only by human agreement, in many cases they require official representations, what I earlier called status indicators, because the existence of institutional facts cannot in general be read off from brute physical facts of the situation. War is an exception for the obvious reason that the brute facts—people killing one another on a large scale, for example—usually make official indicators unnecessary. Money does not require additional documentation, because it is itself a form of documentation. It says on the bill that it is "One Dollar" or "Ten Pounds," etc., and all these terms are defined as money. Even in preliterate societies coins are easily recognizable as such, and thus such features as shape and size mark the conventional fact that the object is a coin. Stocks and bonds, as well as credit cards and checks, also speak for themselves. Likewise, speech acts are self-identifying for those who know the language.

In complex societies common status indicators are passports and driver's licenses. They indicate the status of the bearer as someone who is legally entitled to travel to and from foreign countries or is legally qualified to drive. The most common device for status indication is the written signature. Signing a document may create a new institutional fact, but the continued existence of the written signature indicates, other things being equal, the continued existence of the fact. The signature on the document persists in a way that the live performative does not and thus is able to play its role as a status indicator. The function of status indicators is always *epistemic*. We need to distinguish the role of language in constituting the institutional fact, a role I described in Chapter 3, from the role of language in *identifying* that which has already been constituted, even though the same word or symbol may serve both roles. I am describing this latter role when I speak of status indicators.

Some status indicators need not be explicitly linguistic, that is, they need not be actual words. The most obvious examples are wedding rings and uniforms. But both are nonetheless symbolic in a way that is just like language, and wearing a wedding ring or a uniform is performing a type of speech act. Such indicators serve not only epistemic functions but other functions as well—expressive, ceremonial, aesthetic, and most importantly, constitutive. Of course, the uniform does not constitute being a policeman, but it does symbolize a status-function; and that symbolization, in some form or other, is essential to the existence of the status function. Throughout this book I have tried to emphasize that in institutional facts language is not only descriptive but constitutive of reality.

The Hierarchy of Facts: From Brute to Institutional

There is an implicit hierarchical taxonomy in the account I have been giving, and I would now like to try to make it explicit. The world of Supreme Court decisions and of the collapse of communism is the same world as the world of the formation of planets and of the collapse of the wave function in quantum mechanics. One of the aims of this book is to show how that can be so, how the world of institutions is part of the "physical" world. A hierarchical taxonomy will show the place of the social, institutional, and mental reality within a single physical reality.

However, constructing such a taxonomy is no simple task because several different and crisscrossing distinctions need to be recognized. With some hesitation, I provide a simplified version of the hierarchical relations between the different types of fact in Figure 5.1.

Our original distinction between brute and institutional facts

Figure 5.1

Hierarchical Taxonomy of (Certain Types of) Facts

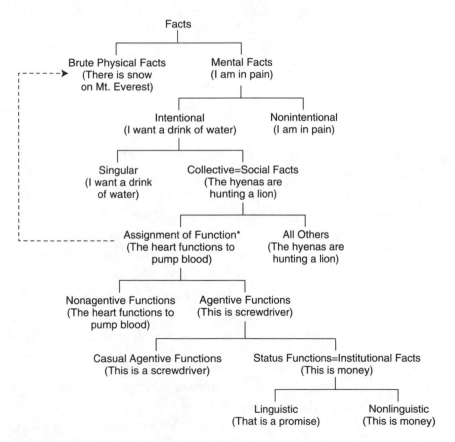

*Functions are always ultimately assigned to brute phenomena, hence the line from the Assignment of Function to Brute Physical Facts.

has now been transcended and must be absorbed within the following further set of distinctions.

AT THE FIRST LEVEL, among the many different sorts of facts, I distinguish between such non mental brute facts as that there is snow and ice at the top of Mt. Everest and mental facts of all kinds, such as the fact that I am in pain or that I want a drink of water. I dislike the old Cartesian terminology, because it seems to imply an opposition between mental and physical, but if we can forget the Cartesian metaphysics, let's call this the distinction between *nonmental brute physical facts* and *mental facts*. I do not mean to imply that these categories exhaust all the kinds of facts. If there are mathematical facts, for example, they would not be included in this taxonomy.

AT THE SECOND LEVEL, within the class of mental facts I distinguish between *intentional facts*, such as the fact that I now want a drink of water, and *nonintentional facts*, such as the fact that I am now in pain.

AT THE THIRD LEVEL, within the class of intentional facts, I distinguish between *singular intentional facts*, such as the fact that I now want a drink of water, and *collective intentional facts*, such as the fact that those hyenas are attacking a lion. By stipulation, I am using the expression "social facts" so that all and only cases of collective intentional facts are social facts. Institutional facts are then a special subclass of social facts, and our problem has been to specify exactly the features that define this subclass.

From now on I will be mostly concerned with social facts, though some of the binary oppositions apply to the singular case as well. For example, there can be both singular and collective imposition of functions on objects.

AT THE FOURTH LEVEL, within both individual and collective intentionality, I distinguish between *those forms of intentionality that assign a function*, as reported by, e.g., "This is a screwdriver," *and all others*, e.g., "I want a drink of water." The assignment of the function creates *functional facts*.

I know it sounds odd to say that the fact that this is a screw-driver is a species of mental fact, that it is ontologically subjective even though epistemically objective; but this consequence follows from the observer-relative character of all functional attributions. Furthermore, since all assignment of function is ultimately on brute facts, this feature of the taxonomy refers back to the existence of brute physical facts in our first level. Sometimes functions can be imposed on other functions, but ultimately such hierarchies must bottom out on brute phenomena. (See Figure 5.1.) In general the hierarchies of assigned functions bottom out on brute "physical" phenomena; but there is no reason in principle why they could not bottom out on mental phenomena. For example, we might decide to count the occurrence of certain mental states as constitutive of certain types of insanity. In such a case X counts as Y, but the X expression refers to a mental phenomenon.

AT THE FIFTH LEVEL, within the class of functional facts I distinguish between *nonagentive functional facts*, e.g., the function of the heart is to pump blood, and *agentive functional facts*, e.g., the function of hammers is to drive nails. Imposed functions are assigned not only to artifacts but also to natural phenomena. Both "That stone makes a good paperweight" and "That is a beautiful sunset" record and assess the imposition of functions on natural phenomena.

Furthermore, just as one can "impose" agentive functions on natural phenomena such as sunsets, so one can "discover" nonagentive functions among artifacts. If, for example, you accept the distinction between manifest and latent functions, and you believe that latent functions are unintended, then the discovery of latent functions of institutions is the discovery of a nonagentive function of an artifact. Thus, for example, if you think that the unintended latent function of money is to maintain a system of oppression, then you will claim to have discovered a nonagentive function among the agentive status-functions of money.

AT THE SIXTH LEVEL, within the category of agentive functions I distinguish between *functions performed solely in virtue of causal*

and other brute features of the phenomena and functions per-
formed only by way of collective acceptance. The key element in
the development of agentive functions into institutional facts
comes when we collectively impose a function on a phenomenon
whose physical composition is insufficient to guarantee the performance of the function, and therefore the function can only be
performed as a matter of collective acceptance or recognition.
These *status-functions* comprise a subcategory of agentive functions. The class of existing status functions is identical with the
class of institutional facts.

Examples of agentive functions performed in virtue of intrinsic
physical structure are reported by "That is a bathtub" and "This is
a screwdriver." Examples of status functions (= institutional facts)
are reported by "That is a twenty dollar bill" and "He is an attorney."

AT THE SEVENTH LEVEL, within the category of status-functions there
are a number of ways of classifying institutional facts. These are
crisscrossing criteria for distinguishing one kind from another. I
cannot get all these on the chart, but here is a list of some of them:

a. We can distinguish institutional facts by subject matter. We
can distinguish among linguistic, economic, political, religious,
etc., institutional facts. For our purposes, the most important distinction in subject matter is between the linguistic and the nonlinguistic, between, for example, the fact that the sentence *"Es
regnet"* means "It's raining" and the fact that Bill Clinton was
elected President of the United States.

b. We can distinguish institutional facts by temporal status. We
can distinguish between the initial creation of an institutional fact
(e.g., Clinton became President in 1993), its continued maintenance (e.g., Clinton was President for all of 1993, Parliament is in
session, etc.) and its eventual cessation through expiration, decay,
or outright destruction (e.g., The Byzantine Empire collapsed in
1453).

c. We can distinguish institutional facts by logical operations. In Chapter 4 I suggested that the basic structure was one of imposed power, according to the structure

We accept (S has power (S does A)).

Such basic structures are reported, for example, by "Sally has twenty dollars" or "Jones is our leader." But there are logical operations such as negation and conditionalization performed on the basic structure. For example, a negation of the power in the content of the institutional fact would be "Sally owes me twenty dollars," and a negation of the acceptance would be reported by "Jones has been removed as leader."

EIGHTH, once we have both linguistic and nonlinguistic institutional functions, we can iterate functions on top of functions. The Y term of one level can be the X term or the C term of the next level up or even of higher levels. Thus such and such an utterance as X1 counts as a promise Y1 in a context C1; but under certain circumstances C2, that very promise, Y1=X2, counts as a legally binding contract, Y2. Given the contract as a context, Y2=C3, a particular action as X3 can count as its breach, Y3. In the context of that breach, Y3=C4, a series of legal actions as X4 may count as a successful lawsuit, Y4, and hence have the function of remedying the breach or compensating for it. Such iterations produce the highest levels of institutional facts.

Institutional Facts and the Background of Capacities

I have sometimes spoken as if the collective imposition of functions were always a matter of a deliberate act or set of actions. But except for special cases where legislation is passed or the authorities change the rules of a game, the creation of institutional facts is typically a matter of natural evolution, and there need be no explicit conscious imposition of function—whether status or other type of function—on lower-level phenomena. The story that I told about money illustrates this point. Money gradually evolves in ways that we are not aware of. It is not the case that one fine day we all decided to count bits of paper as money; rather, the form that the collective intentionality takes is that we begin to accept such promissory notes as media of exchange, and we continue collectively to accept them. Some cases involve explicit intentionality, but that seems to me only one type of case. One way to impose a function on an object is just to start using the object to perform that function. The presuppositions of the *use* of entities that have a function are often in the form of Background phenomena that are simply taken for granted.

Furthermore even in cases where the function is assigned in collective acts of intentional imposition, the subsequent use of the entities in question need not contain the intentionality of the original imposition. One person, or perhaps a group of people, invent tools, say, screwdrivers and hammers, for example. In such a case, they create types of devices on which they impose a certain function by collective intentionality. But subsequent generations are simply brought up in a culture containing screwdrivers and hammers. They never think about the imposition of collective intentionality; they simply take it for granted that these are certain types of useful tools. What was once the explicit imposition of function in a collective intentional act is now assumed as part of the Background. In Chapter 6 we will explore the Background and its relation to causal explanations of social phenomena.

6

Background Abilities and the Explanation of Social Phenomena

Constitutive Rules and Causation

I have said that the structure of human institutions is a structure of constitutive rules. I have also said that people who are participating in the institutions are typically not conscious of these rules; often they even have false beliefs about the nature of the institution, and even the very people who created the institution may be unaware of its structure. But this combination of claims poses a serious question for us: Under these conditions, what causal role can such rules possibly play in the actual behavior of those who are participating in the institutions? If the people who are participating in the institution are not conscious of the rules and do not appear to be trying to follow them, either consciously or unconsciously, and if indeed the very people who created or participated

127

in the evolution of the institution may themselves have been totally ignorant of the system of rules, then what causal role could the rules play?

The rules are in general not codified, and even in cases such as natural language and property where linguists, legislators, and lawyers have codified many of the rules, most of us are unaware of these codifications. And even if we were aware, the codifications are not self-interpreting. We have to know how to interpret or apply the codified rules.

A standard answer to this question is given in the literature of cognitive science and linguistics. I will be rejecting this answer in the course of this chapter. The answer is: Of course we are following these rules, but we do so *unconsciously.* Indeed, in many cases the rules are not even the sort of rules that we *could* be conscious of. For example, Chomsky, in his account of Universal Grammar, says that the child is able to learn the grammar of a particular natural language only because he or she already is innately in possession of the rules of a Universal Grammar, and these rules are so deeply unconscious that there is no way that a child could become conscious of their operation.[1] This move is very common in cognitive science. Fodor says that to understand any language we all have to know the Language of Thought.[2] And this language is so deeply unconscious that we can never become conscious of its operation. I am very dissatisfied with these accounts. Since Freud we have found it useful and convenient to speak glibly about the unconscious mind without paying the price of explaining exactly what we mean. Our picture of unconscious mental states is that they are just like conscious states only minus the consciousness. But what exactly is that supposed to mean? I have not seen a satisfactory answer to that question—certainly not in Chomsky or Fodor and not even in Freud. To put the point crudely, I believe that in most appeals to the unconscious in Cognitive Science we really have no clear idea what we are talking about.[3]

However, in this chapter I am not primarily interested in the limitations of our current explanatory models but in proposing an alternative form of explanation. To explain how we can relate to rule structures such as language, property, money, marriage, and so on, in cases where we do not know the rules and are not following them either consciously or unconsciously, I have to appeal to the notion that I have elsewhere called "the Background."[4] This chapter has two parts. In the first part I will make some general remarks about the Background and how it works; in the second part I will apply the principles stated in the first part to the understanding of institutional reality.

What Is the Background and How Does It Work?

In my writings on issues in the philosophy of mind and the philosophy of language, I have argued for what I call the thesis of the Background: Intentional states function only given a set of Background capacities that do not themselves consist in intentional phenomena. Thus, for example, beliefs, desires, and rules only determine conditions of satisfaction—truth conditions for beliefs, fulfillment conditions for desires, etc.—given a set of capacities that do not themselves consist in intentional phenomena. I have thus defined the concept of the "Background" as the set of nonintentional or preintentional capacities that enable intentional states of function. But in that definition there are four difficult concepts: "capacities," "enabling," "intentional states," and "function."

By *capacities* I mean abilities, dispositions, tendencies, and *causal structures generally*. It is important to see that when we talk about the Background we are talking about a certain category of neurophysiological causation. Because we do not know how these structures function at a neurophysiological level, we are forced to describe them at a much higher level. There is nothing disreputable about that. When I say, for example, that I am able to speak English, I am talking about a causal capacity of my brain; but there is no objection to identifying that capacity as, e.g., "the ability to speak English" without knowing the details of its neurophysiological realization.

Enabling is meant, then, to be a causal notion. We are not talking about logical conditions of possibility but about neurophysiological structures that function causally in the production of certain sorts of intentional phenomena.

Intentional states: I will assume that intentionality is unproblematic for the sake of this discussion, though I realize it is in fact a matter of much debate. Specifically, I am going to assume that my arguments to show that all intentional states are either actually or potentially conscious are sound[5] and therefore I will confine my discussion to conscious forms of intentionality.

Finally, *function:* We will see shortly that there is a variety of different types of functioning of the Background. I will try to explain these under the general heading of the varieties of enabling.

The simplest argument for the thesis of the Background is that the literal meaning of any sentence can only determine its truth conditions or other conditions of satisfaction against a Background of capacities, dispositions, know-how, etc., which are not themselves part of the semantic content of the sentence. You can see this if you think about any sentence at all, but it is perhaps most obvious with sentences containing simple English verbs like "cut," "open," or "grow." Think, for example, of the occurrence of the word "cut" in sentences such as "Sally cut the cake" or "Bill cut the grass" or "The tailor cut the cloth"; or think of the verb "grow" in sentences such as "The American economy is growing" or "My son is growing" or "The grass is growing." In a normal literal utterance of each of these sentences, each verb has a constant meaning. There is no lexical ambiguity or metaphorical usage involved. But in each case the same verb will determine different truth conditions or conditions of satisfaction generally, because what counts as cutting or growing will vary with the context. If you consider the sentence "Cut the grass!" you know that this is to be interpreted differently from "Cut the cake!" If somebody tells me to cut the cake and I run over it with a lawn mower or they tell me to cut the grass and I rush and stab it with a knife, there is a very ordinary sense in which I did not do what I was told to do. Yet nothing in the literal meaning of those sentences blocks those wrong interpretations. In each case we understand the verb differently, even though its literal meaning is constant, because in each case our interpretation depends on our Background abilities.

I do not want now to develop the argument in favor of the Background, but I do want to emphasize that the phenomenon is pervasive. Consider an example of the sorts of sentences that are discussed in linguistic pragmatics: "She gave him her key and he opened the door." There is much discussion about whether when a speaker utters that sentence it is actually said (or merely implied) that he opened the door *with that key,* and whether he actually says that she *first* gave him the key and *then later* he opened the door; but it is generally agreed that there is a certain underdetermination of what is said by the literal meaning of this sentence.[6] I wish to say that there is a *radical* underdetermination of what is said by the literal meaning of the sentence. There is nothing in the literal meaning of the sentence "She gave him her key and he opened the door" to block the interpretation, He opened the door with her key by bashing the door down with the key; the key weighed two hundred pounds and was in the shape of an axe. Or, He swallowed both the door and the key and he inserted the key in the lock by the peristaltic contraction of his gut.

I leave it to your imagination to produce an indefinite range of ridiculous but still literal interpretations of this or any other sentence. And the point is that the only thing that blocks those interpretations is not the semantic content but simply the fact that you have a certain sort of knowledge about how the world works, you have a certain set of abilities for coping with the world, and those abilities are not and could not be included as part of the literal meaning of the sentence.

The thesis of the Background can be extended from semantic contents to intentional contents generally. Any intentional state only functions, that is, it only determines conditions of satisfaction, against a set of Background abilities, dispositions, and capacities that are not part of the intentional content and could not be included as part of the content.

My discussion of the Background is related to other discussions in contemporary philosophy. I think that much of Wittgenstein's later work is about what I call the Background. And if I understand him correctly, Pierre Bourdieu's important work on the "habitus" is about the same sort of phenomena that I call the Background. In the history of philosophy, I believe Hume was the first philosopher to recognize the centrality of the Background in explaining human cognition, and Nietzsche was the philosopher most impressed by its radical contingency. Nietzsche saw, with anxiety, that the Background does not have to be the way it is.

How does the Background work? I want to give you a feel for how Background capacities, though they are not and could not be construed as further intentional contents, nonetheless form the necessary preconditions for the functioning of intentional contents. One way to do this is to list several types of Background functions.

First, as already argued, the Background enables linguistic interpretation to take place.

I have claimed that the meaning of any sentence radically underdetermines its truth conditions, because the literal meaning of the sentence only fixes a set of truth conditions given certain Background capacities. Notice that in the examples the words have a common semantic content. The word "cut" does keep a common meaning in our examples, but we don't interpret the sentences at the level of bare semantic content; interpretation rises to the level of our Background abilities. We immediately and effortlessly interpret these sentences in the stereotypical appropriate way.

Second, the Background enables perceptual interpretation to take place.

What goes for semantics goes for perception. It is a familiar point that given certain Background skills, we are able to see things as certain sorts of things. Remember Wittgenstein's example of the figure that can be seen as either a duck looking to the left or a rabbit looking to the right, up at the sky.[7] We are able to see the figure as either a duck or a rabbit, because we bring to bear on the raw perceptual stimulus a set of Background skills; in this case we bring the ability to apply certain categories. And what goes for this case goes for perception in general. I see this as a chair, this as a table, that as a glass, indeed any normal case of perception will be a case of *perceiving as,* where the perceiver assimilates the perceived object to some more or less familiar category.

These two pervasive functions, namely, the role of the Background in facilitating linguistic interpretation and the role in facilitating perceptual interpretation, are extended to consciousness generally:

Third, the Background structures consciousness.

It is an interesting fact about consciousness that our conscious experiences come to us with what we might call an aspect of familiarity. Even if I am in a strange locale, in the jungles of Mexico or in Africa, though the houses and the dress of the people look different from the way they look in Europe or in the United States still, those are familiar to me as houses and those are familiar as people; this is clothing; that is the sky; this is the earth. All non-pathological forms of consciousness are experienced under the aspect of familiarity. And this is a function of our Background capacities. Because all intentionality is aspectual, all conscious intentionality is aspectual; and the possibility of perceiving, that is, the possibility of experiencing under aspects requires a familiarity with the set of categories under which one experiences those aspects. The ability to apply those categories is a Background ability.

We find this third feature of the Background by extending the first two features, namely, the features that the Background is essential to semantic interpretation and to perceptual interpretation. I am reluctant to use the word "interpretation" because it suggests something that is definitely false. The use of this word suggests that there is an act of interpreting whenever we understand something or perceive something, and of course I don't want to say that. I want to say we normally just see an object or understand a sentence, without any *act* of interpreting. It is a very special intellectual performance to produce an act of interpretation. With Wittgenstein[8] I might want to reserve the word "interpretation" for cases where we actually perform a conscious and deliberate act of interpreting, e.g., where we substitute one expression for another. With that caveat, I want to say that the understanding of utterances and the experiencing of ordinary conscious states require Background capacities.

Notice the sheer intellectual effort it takes to break with our Background. Surrealist painters tried to do this, but even in a surrealist painting, the three-headed woman is still a woman, and the drooping watch is still a watch, and those crazy objects are still objects against a horizon, with a sky and a foreground.

I apologize for the swiftness with which I am moving through this dangerous territory. I am trying as quickly as I can to get back to the main question of the causal explanations of institutional facts, and right now the point is to develop the tools I need for that discussion.

This leads to the next manifestation of the Background.

Fourth, temporally extended sequences of experiences come to us with a narrative or dramatic shape. They come to us under what for want of a better word I will call "dramatic" categories.

Just as our particular experiences occur to us as aspectual, i.e., with aspectual shapes, so there is a narrative shape to sequences of experiences. The Background has not only an episodic application, as in the examples that we have so far considered, but it also has what we might call a dynamic application over a series of successive events. Obvious instances of this are where the perceptual and linguistic categories extend to long sequences of events. I not only perceive things as houses, cars, and people but I also possess certain scenarios of expectation that enable me to cope with the people and objects in my environment; and these include a set of categories for how houses, cars, and people interact, or how things proceed when I walk into a restaurant, or what happens when I shop in a supermarket, for example. More grandly, people have a series of expectations about bigger categories in their life, such as the category of falling in love, or getting married and raising a family, or going to a university and getting a degree. La Rochefoucauld says somewhere that very few people would fall in love if they never read about it; and nowadays, we would have to add if they never saw it on television or in the movies. What they get from television, movies, and reading is, of course, in part a set of beliefs and desires. The point at present, however, is that beliefs and desires only fix conditions of satisfaction against a Background of capacities that are not themselves beliefs or desires. So another manifestation of the Background is in what I call the dramatic categories that extend over sequences of events and structure those sequences into narrative shapes.

Fifth, each of us has a set of motivational dispositions, and these will condition the structure of our experiences.

Let us suppose that you are obsessed by Oriental rugs, sports cars, and fine wines. Then you will experience the streets of Paris or New York in a different way from the person who is obsessed by cloud formations and Arizona cactus. There are lots of opportunities for the collector of fine wines and Oriental rugs, not so much for Arizona cactus. Of course, collectors of Oriental rugs do have conscious beliefs and desires about Oriental rugs. I believe that Kazaks cost a lot more than Hamadans, for example, and I believe that all antique rugs nowadays cost too much. I would like to own a Chi-Chi. These and other beliefs and desires help to structure my experiences. But the important thing for the present discussion is that, in addition to such specific beliefs and desires, what gives sense to those beliefs and desires is a set of motivational dispositions.

Sixth, the Background facilitates certain kinds of readiness.

At any given point I am ready for certain things and not other things. In large cities, I am ready for street noises, I am ready for the sound of cars and the sights of lots of other people, stores, and traffic. When I am on the ski slope, I am ready for other skiers coming by as potential projectiles. But when I am giving a lecture I am not at all ready for a skier to come skiing through the lecture hall; I would be absolutely astounded if a skier suddenly came through, or if an elephant simply walked into the room. But I am completely ready for the sorts of noises and responses that one normally hears in lecture halls. My Background capacities determine a set of readinesses that structure the nature of my experience. When I am skiing, I am ready for other skiers as potential sources of danger, as people likely to try to push in front of me in the lift line, as exemplars of good skiing technique, as attractive members of the opposite sex, as wearers of good or bad ski apparel, as old skiing friends I encounter on the ski slope. In a seminar, I am ready for people to raise their hand and accuse me of infinite regress arguments or fallacies of composition, but I do not have the reverse readiness. If in the deep snow at the top of Red Dog Ridge, I encountered a bunch of people seated at university desks, raising their hands and saying such things to me as "There is an infinite regress in one of your arguments," I would be astounded by that. Such things could happen, but they definitely are not the sort of thing that the Background makes me ready for. A lot of comedy is based on just such incongruities.

Seventh, the Background disposes me to certain sorts of behavior.

I am disposed to laugh at certain kinds of jokes and not others, I am disposed to speak at a certain level of loudness and not at another, I am disposed to stand at a certain distance from people when I talk to them and not at certain other distances. I am calling all of these, manifestations of the Background.

These, then, are seven ways in which my Background abilities manifest themselves in actual occurrent forms of intentionality. I do not for a moment suppose that these are all the ways that the Background is manifested, but at least they are ones I feel reasonably confident fit the theory of the Background that I have tried to state so far.

Background Causation

Now I turn to my main topic: How can it be that the rules of the institution play a role in our dealings with the institution, even though we are not following the rules either consciously or unconsciously? Of course, in some cases we actually are following the rules. I might teach you a new card game and you might memorize the rules and follow the rules of the game. But for many institutions, particularly after I have become expert at operating within the institution, I just know what to do. I know what the appropriate behavior is, without reference to the rules.

Let me give a couple of examples of what puzzles me. Consider the skilled professional playing baseball. After he hits the ball he runs to first base. Now if we ask, Why does he do that? we can say: He wants to get a hit; he wants to get on first base; he wants to do that because he wants to score runs; and he wants to score runs so that his team can win. But what role do the rules of baseball play in this explanation? Do we also want to say that he wants to follow the rules of baseball? That seems a little odd; that is more appropriate to the beginner. Unless there is some dispute, the rules of baseball don't concern the expert at all; he is too far advanced to be worried about the rules of baseball. Consider another example. A woman takes her shopping list to the supermarket. The list is an explicit statement of a set of desires, and in the course of the shopping the woman will be dealing with money and merchandise. Do we want to say that in addition to the desire for the items she is buying, she has a desire to follow the constitutive rules of money or that she is unconsciously following the constitutive rules of money? I find those claims implausible. And that implausibility leads me to the questions I am now trying to pose.

If we look at the recent history of the social sciences, we find roughly speaking that two kinds of causation are accepted. One is mental causation, according to which the agent is operating consciously or unconsciously, with a set of rational procedures over more or less well-defined sets of intentional states, such as preference schedules or internalized rules. There are many cases in which that sort of intentionalistic explanation is appropriate, where, for example, we have rational decision making in behavior. This happens, for example, when the leaders of a country try to decide on an economic policy that will improve the balance of payments and the rate of economic growth. That is a case of rational decision making, and something like the principles of rational decision making seem to apply. But there are also many cases where that model is very unnatural. Suppose I am driving to work, or suppose I am sitting in a restaurant looking at the menu and trying to decide what to eat. In such cases it seems implausible to say that I am performing a set of calculations to try to get myself on a higher indifference curve, given an antecedent set of well-ordered preferences.

In fact, if you look really closely at decision theoretic models of rationality, you will find that they are not satisfactory at all. Here is one example. It is a consequence of Bayesian decision theory that if you value any two things, there must be some odds at which you would bet one against the other. Thus if you value a dime and you value your life, there must be some odds at which you would bet your life against a dime. Now I have to tell you, there are no odds at which I would bet my life for a dime, or if there were, there are certainly no odds at which I would bet my son's life for a dime. I have pointed this out to several famous decision theorists, and after usually half an hour of argument, they say, "You are simply irrational." I do not think so. I think it is rather they who have a problem with rationality. This is not the place to develop the argument, but I want to suggest that a conception of rationality as a set of specific, well-defined operations over sharply delineated, explicit intentional contents is inadequate.

Another form of causal explanation that is common in the social sciences does not appeal to intentional contents but to brute physical causation. In the United States, behaviorism was the most prominent version of this type of explanation. I had thought that behaviorism was dead, but there are some recent efforts to revive it.

How then should we think of Background causation? If we think there are these two general models of causation of behavior, one employing intentional causation and one employing what could be called billiard-ball causation, which is the appropriate model for describing the Background? I shall argue that in the end neither is an appropriate model. We need a different model for explaining how Background abilities enable us to relate to institutions.

Readers familiar with recent debates in cognitive science will recognize certain closely related problems. My problem is, How do we characterize the role of Background capacities for dealing with institutions? A related problem that has been discussed for decades concerns how to distinguish between rule-*described* behavior and rule-*governed* behavior. How are we to think of the rules of a language, for example, the rules of a syntax? On one view, we should just say that the rules do not have any reality except as a part of a theoretical description of phenomena. So the rules are a device the linguist uses to characterize the phenomena, but they just describe the behavior, they don't actually play any role in causing it. The more adventurous view says that the behavior isn't just rule-described but is rule-governed, or rule-guided. And in this case we are to think of the semantic content of the rule as actually playing a causal role in determining the behavior. So that when the agent, for example, produces an English sentence, her unconscious internalization of the rules is actually acting causally to produce that particular syntactic structure. And when the mature adult performs speech acts, in any language, when she makes a promise or gives an order, we are to think of the rules of speech acts as functioning unconsciously in the production of the behavior.

Now, which of those is the right way to think of the Background? I am not satisfied with either. Here is the problem as I see it. If we think of the Background intentionalistically, then we have abandoned the thesis of the Background. We arrived at that thesis in the first place only because we found that intentionality goes only so far. The intentionality is not self-interpreting. But if, on the other hand, we say that the rules play no causal role at all in the behavior, then we must say that the Background is such that this is just what the person does, he just behaves that way. For example, he produces these kinds of sentences and not other kinds. He simply acts the way he does, and that is the end of the story. Wittgenstein often talks in this latter way. He says there just is an *ungrounded* way of acting.[9] We reach the point where we just do it. We talk this way and not that way. We accept this and not that. But Wittgenstein's approach is very unsatisfying, because it does not tell us what the role of the rule structure is. We want to say that institutions like money, property, syntax, and speech acts are systems of constitutive rules, and we want to know the role of that rule structure in the causal explanation of human behavior. I talk and I buy things with money as naturally as I walk, but talk and money seem to have a rule structure that walking does not seem to have.

Another way in which a closely related issue comes out in contemporary intellectual life is in the current debate between the two competing paradigms in cognitive science. One is the paradigm of the traditional, von Neumann serial information processing, where a computer implements a set of linear steps of a program. The other is the more recent development of parallel distributed processing, or neuronal net modeling, where there is a meaningful input and a meaningful output, but in between there are no symbol-processing steps; rather, there is just a series of nodes with different connection strengths between them, and signals pass from one node to another, and eventually changes in the connection strengths give the right match of inputs and outputs, without any set of rules or logical principles in between. One might say that this whole talk about the Background is certainly more in tune with, is more sympathetic with, the connectionist model of cognition. I think that's right. But it still leaves us with the challenge posed by those who oppose connectionism, namely, what are the features of the internal structure that enable the system to produce a structured output that manifests compositional and other logical properties?

Here is our paradox: We want a causal explanation that will explain the intricacy, the complexity, and the sensitivity of our behavior as well as explaining its spontaneity, creativity, and originality. But we only have the two paradigms of causal explanation, and neither seems adequate to explain the relations of individual humans to social structures. One is the paradigm of rational decision making according to rules, principles, and the like, and the other is brute physical causation and therefore non-intentionalistic and not rationalistic. Whether it is connectionism or behaviorism, this type of causation does not have a rational structure.

The key to understanding the causal relations between the structure of the Background and the structure of social institutions is to see that the Background can be causally sensitive to the specific forms of the constitutive rules of the institutions without actually containing any beliefs or desires or representations of those rules. To see this, let us start with a simple example. Suppose a baseball player learns how to play baseball. At the beginning he actually learns a set of rules, principles, and strategies. But after he gets skilled, his behavior becomes much more fluent, much more melodic, much more responsive to the demands of the situation. In such a case, it seems to me, he is not applying the rules more skillfully; rather, he has acquired a set of dispositions or skills to respond appropriately, where the appropriateness is actually determined by the structure of the rules, strategies, and principles of baseball. The basic idea, which I will now explain, is that one can develop, one can evolve, a set of abilities that are sensitive to specific structures of intentionality without actually being constituted by that intentionality. One develops skills and abilities that are, so to speak, functionally equivalent to the system of rules, without actually containing any representations or internalizations of those rules.

Consider a slightly more complicated case than baseball, consider money. I have tried to describe some of the constitutive rules of money. How do those rules function in actual behavior? The users of money do not know those rules, and in general, I am arguing, they do not apply them consciously or unconsciously; rather, they have developed a set of dispositions that are sensitive and responsive to the specific content of those rules. So they must have the ability to use money as a medium of exchange, and they have to be responsive to the distinction between counterfeit money and real money, even though they might not be able to tell the difference without expert help. Their behavior has to be responsive to the fact that currency is valuable not because of the paper it is printed on but because it functions as a medium of exchange. And those sorts of abilities, this type of know-how, that become ingrained are in fact a reflection of the sets of constitutive rules whereby we impose functions on entities that do not have those functions in virtue of their physical structure, but acquire the function only through collective agreement or acceptance.

There is a parallelism between the functional structure of the Background and the intentional structure of the social phenomena to which the Background capacities relate. That strict parallelism gives us the illusion that the person who is able to deal with money, to cope with society, and speak a language must be unconsciously following rules. Here I am arguing, Of course there are rules and often we do follow them, both consciously and unconsciously, but

1. The rules are never self interpreting,

and

2. They are never exhaustive,

and

3. In fact in many situations, we just know what to do, we just know how to deal with the situation. We do not apply the rules consciously or unconsciously.

We don't stop and think, consciously or unconsciously, "Ah ha! Money is a case of the imposition of function through collective intentionality according to a rule of the form 'X counts as Y in C' and requires collective agreement." Rather, we develop skills that are responsive to that particular institutional structure.

We can understand these points better if we consider some analogous explanatory strategies. There is an obvious analogy between what I have been saying and certain problems in evolutionary biology. From a philosophical point of view, the marvelous thing about Darwinian evolutionary biology was not only that it drove teleology out of the biological explanation of the origin of species but that it gave us a new kind of explanation, a form of explanation that inverts the order of the explanatory apparatus. So, in pre-Darwinian biology, we would say, for example, "The fish has the shape that it does in order to survive in water." In evolutionary biology we perform an inversion on that intentional or teleological explanation, where we substitute two levels of explanation. First, the causal level: We say the fish has the shape that it has because of its genetic structure, because of the way the genotype, in response to the environment, produces the phenotype. Second, the "functional" level: We say that fish that have that shape are more likely to survive than fish that do not. Thus, we have inverted the structure of the explanation. The original structure was, the fish has this shape in order to survive; now we have inverted it: the fish is going to have this shape anyway, but fish that do have this shape are more likely to survive than fish that do not. Notice what we have done in the inversion. Survival still functions as part of the explanation, but now it is introduced into the explanation diachronically. It functions over a period of many generations, and its causal role is inverted. Because the teleology is now eliminated, survival is not a goal that is pursued but simply an effect that happens; and when it happens it enables the reproduction of the survival-producing mechanisms.

A similar inversion should be applied to human Background capacities for coping with social phenomena. Instead of saying, the person behaves the way he does because he is following the rules of the institution, we should just say, First (the causal level), the person behaves the way he does, because he has a structure that disposes him to behave that way; and second (the functional level), he has come to be disposed to behave that way, because that's the way that conforms to the rules of the institution.

In other words, he doesn't need to know the rules of the institution and to follow them in order to conform to the rules; rather, he is just disposed to behave in a certain way, but he has acquired those unconscious dispositions and capacities in a way that is sensitive to the rule structure of the institution. To tie this down to a concrete case, we should not say that the experienced baseball player runs to first base because he wants to follow the rules of baseball, but we should say that because the rules require that he run to first base, he acquires a set of Background habits, skills, dispositions that are such that when he hits the ball, he runs to first base.

Let me give a thought experiment that will illustrate the line of explanation I am proposing. Suppose there were a tribe where children just grew up playing baseball. They never learn the rules as codified rules but are rewarded or criticized for doing the right thing or the wrong thing. For example, if the child has three strikes, and he says "Can't I have another chance?" he is told, "No, now you have to sit down and let someone else come up to bat." We can suppose that the children just become very skillful at playing baseball. Now also suppose that a foreign anthropologist tries to describe the culture of the tribe. A good anthropologist might come up with the rules of baseball just by describing the behavior of these people and what they regard as normative in baseball situations. But it does not follow from the accuracy of the anthropological description that the members of this society are consciously or unconsciously following those rules. Nonetheless, those rules do play a crucial role in the explanation of their behavior, because they have acquired the dispositions that they have, precisely because those are the rules of baseball.

This was intended as a fantasy example, but in real life we are in a very similar situation regarding the rules of syntax or the rules of speech acts. Only someone who is a speech act theorist, as I am, would ever bother to codify the rules of speech acts. As the child grows up she finds out, for example, that if she makes a promise, she has to keep it, and if she breaks it she is severely criticized. The child acquires a certain know-how that enables her to cope with the institution. And what goes for baseball and promising seems to me to go for syntax as well. I am proposing, then, that in learning to cope with social reality, we acquire a set of cognitive abilities that are everywhere sensitive to an intentional structure, and in particular to the rule structures of complex institutions, without necessarily everywhere containing representations of the rules of those institutions.

To summarize: We can acknowledge the extremely complex, rule-governed structures of human institutions, and we can also acknowledge that those rule-governed structures play a causal role in the structure of our behavior, but I want to propose that in many cases it is just wrong to assume, and certainly unsupported by the evidence that has been presented in the course of these discussions, that our behavior matches the structure of the rules because we are unconsciously following the rules. Rather, we evolve a set of dispositions that are sensitive to the rule structure.

Somebody might object, "Aren't you really saying that it is 'as if' we were following the rules. But then that doesn't really explain anything, since if there is no real intentionality, the 'as if' intentionality doesn't explain anything. As-if intentionality has no causal power because it does not really exist. As-if intentionality is just as empty as Daniel Dennett's 'intentional stance'[10] and all of that is precisely the sort of behaviorism you have been militating against."

No, that is not what I am saying; rather, I am saying that if you understand the complexity of the causation involved, you can see that often the person who behaves in a skillful way within an institution behaves as if he were following the rules, but not because he is following the rules unconsciously nor because his behavior is caused by an undifferentiated mechanism that happens to look as if it were rule structured, but rather because *the mechanism has evolved precisely so that it will be sensitive to the rules.* The mechanism explains the behavior, and the mechanism is explained by the system of rules, but the mechanism need not itself be a system of rules. I am in short urging the addition of another level, a diachronic level, in the explanation of certain sorts of social behavior.

Now, one last objection. Somebody might say, "Why do you have these rules at all? Why don't you just have some kind of behaviorism? These things just happen, people just do these things." The answer is that where human institutions are concerned, we accept a socially created normative component. We accept that there is something wrong with the person who when the baseball is pitched at him simply eats it; something wrong with the person who doesn't recognize any reason to do something after he has made a promise to do it; something wrong with the person who goes around spouting ungrammatical sentences. And all these cases involve something wrong in a way that is different from the way there is something wrong with the man who stumbles when he walks; that is, there is a socially created normative component in the institutional structure, and this is accounted for only by the fact that the institutional structure is a structure of rules, and the actual rules that we specify in describing the institution will determine those aspects under which the system is normative. It is precisely because of the rule that making a promise counts as undertaking an obligation that we recognize that certain kinds of behavior within the institution of promising are acceptable and certain other kinds are remiss. So there are in fact constitutive rules functioning causally, and we do in fact discover those rules in the course of our analysis. But it does not follow that a person is able to function in a society only if he has actually learned and memorized the rules and is following them consciously or unconsciously. Nor does it follow that a person is able to function in society only if he has "internalized" the rules *as rules.* The point is that we should not say that the man who is at home in his society, the man who is *chez lui* in the social institutions of the society, is at home because he has mastered the rules of the society, but rather that the man has developed a set of capacities and abilities that render him at home in the society; and he has developed those abilities because those are the rules of his society. The man at home in his society is as comfortable as the fish in the sea or the eyeball in its socket, and we do not have to account for the behavior entirely in terms of rules in any of these three cases.

7

Does the Real World Exist?

Part I: Attacks on Realism

So far I have tried to analyze the nature and structure of those facts that, in a sense I attempted to explain, are dependent on human agreement or acceptance. The whole analysis presupposes a distinction between facts dependent on us and those that exist independently of us, a distinction I originally characterized as one between social and institutional facts on the one hand and brute facts on the other. It is now time to defend the contrast on which the analysis rests, to defend the idea that there is a reality totally independent of us. Furthermore, throughout the book I have been presupposing that in general our statements when true correspond to facts, and it is now also time to defend this presupposition. These defenses are made more pressing by the current philosophical scene in which it is common both to deny the existence of a reality independent of human representations and to deny that true statements correspond to facts. This chapter and the next are about realism; the final chapter is about the correspondence theory of truth. A thorough discussion of these problems would require at least another book, but for the purposes of this book I need at least a brief exposition of certain presuppositions behind our contemporary commonsense scientific world view because the rest of this book, not to mention that world view, depends on these presuppositions. These last three chapters are efforts at philosophical housekeeping, trying to clean up the mess, so to speak.

Some Presuppositions of Our Contemporary World View

In order to understand what is at stake, we need to get some of the presuppositions of our world view out into the open, where we can have a look at them. A formal feature of our world view is the distinction between objectivity and subjectivity that I tried to explain in Chapter 1. In addition to the usual problems of vagueness and marginal cases—problems that are not serious—this distinction is systematically ambiguous between an epistemic and an ontological sense. In light of the distinction between epistemic objectivity/subjectivity and ontological objectivity/subjectivity, we can identify the following structural features of our world view.

1. The world (or alternatively, reality or the universe) exists independently of our representations of it. This view I will call "external realism." I will refine its formulation later.

2. Human beings have a variety of interconnected ways of having access to and representing features of the world to themselves. These include perception, thought, language, beliefs, and desires as well as pictures, maps, diagrams, etc. Just to have a general term I will call these collectively "representations." A feature

of representations so defined is that they all have intentionality, both *intrinsic* intentionality, as in beliefs and perceptions, and *derived* intentionality, as in maps and sentences.

3. Some of those representations, such as beliefs and statements, purport to be about and to represent how things are in reality. To the extent that they succeed or fail, they are said to be true or false, respectively. They are true if and only if they correspond to the facts in reality. This is (a version of) the correspondence theory of truth.

4. Systems of representation, such as vocabularies and conceptual schemes generally, are human creations, and to that extent arbitrary. It is possible to have any number of different systems of representations for representing the same reality. This thesis is called "conceptual relativity." Again, I will refine its formulation later.

5. Actual human efforts to get true representations of reality are influenced by all sorts of factors—cultural, economic, psychological, and so on. Complete epistemic objectivity is difficult, sometimes impossible, because actual investigations are always from a point of view, motivated by all sorts of personal factors, and within a certain cultural and historical context.

6. Having knowledge consists in having true representations for which we can give certain sorts of justification or evidence. Knowledge is thus by definition objective in the epistemic sense, because the criteria for knowledge are not arbitrary, and they are impersonal.

Knowledge can be naturally classified by subject matter, but there is no special subject matter called "science" or "scientific knowledge." There is just knowledge, and "science" is a name we apply to areas where knowledge has become systematic, as in physics or chemistry.

In light of the distinction between the epistemic and ontological senses of the objective/subjective distinction, we can say: Proposition 1 (external realism) is very close to the view that there is an ontologically objective reality. The two claims are not exactly equivalent, because the claim that there is a reality independent of representations (external realism) is not exactly equivalent to the claim that there is a reality completely independent of minds (ontological objectivity). The reason for this distinction is that some mental states, such as pains, are ontologically subjective, but they are not representations. They are representation independent but not mind independent. Ontological objectivity implies external realism, because mind independence implies representation independence. But not conversely. Pains, for example, can be representation independent without being mind independent. Proposition 2 implies that ontological subjectivity gives us epistemic access to all the reality to which we have access, whether ontologically subjective or objective, whether epistemically subjective or objective. Proposition 5 says epistemic objectivity is often hard to obtain; and Proposition 6 says that if we have genuine knowledge, we have epistemic objectivity *by definition.*

I hope the reader finds these six propositions so obvious as to wonder why I am boring him or her with such platitudes, but I have to report that a great deal of confusion surrounds them. Propositions 1 and 3, realism and the correspondence theory, respectively, are often confused with each other; worse yet, they are both often supposed to have been refuted. Several philosophers think that proposition 4, conceptual relativity, creates a problem for realism; some think that it refutes it. Many philosophers think that proposition 3, the correspondence theory, has been independently refuted. Several literary theorists think that proposition 5 creates a problem for the very possibility of objective knowledge as stated in proposition 6, and perhaps even refutes realism as articulated by proposition 1.

So I fear there is nothing to do but slow down and go over at least some of these matters in low gear. Let us begin by asking,

What Is Realism?

As a preliminary formulation, I have defined realism as the view that the world exists independently of our representations of it. This has the consequence that if we had never existed, if there had never been any representations—any statements, beliefs, perceptions, thoughts, etc.—most of the world would have remained unaffected. Except for the little corner of the world that is constituted or affected by our representations, the world would still have existed and would have been exactly the same as it is now. It has the further consequence that when we all die, and all our representations die with us, most features of the world will remain totally unaffected; they will go on exactly as before. For example, let us assume that there is a mountain in the Himalayas that I represent to myself and others as "Mount Everest." Mount Everest exists independently of how or whether I or anyone else ever represented it or anything else. Furthermore, there are many features of Mount Everest, for example, the sort of features that I represent if I make a statement such as "Mt. Everest has snow and ice near its summit," which would have remained totally unaffected if no one had ever represented them in any fashion and will not be affected by the demise of these or any other representations. One might put this point by saying that there are many language-independent features, facts, states of affairs, etc.; but I have put the point more generally in terms of "representations," because I want to note that the world exists independently not only of language but also of thought, perception, belief, etc. The point is that, in large part, reality does not depend on intentionality in any form.

In the history of philosophy the word "realism" has been used with a wide variety of meanings. In the medieval sense, realism is the doctrine that universals have a real existence. Nowadays one hears talk of "modal realism," "ethical realism," "intentional realism," "mathematical realism," and so on. For the purposes of this discussion I am stipulating that "external realism" and "realism"

("ER" for short) name the view sketched in the previous paragraph. I use the metaphor of "external" to mark the fact that the view in question holds that reality exists outside of, or external to, our system of representation.

Before examining arguments for and against realism we need to distinguish it from other views with which it is often identified. The first confusion is to suppose that realism is identical with or at least implies the correspondence theory of truth. But realism is not a theory of truth and it does not imply any theory of truth. Strictly speaking, realism is consistent with any theory of truth because it is a theory of ontology and not of the meaning of "true." It is not a semantic theory at all. It is thus possible to hold ER and deny the correspondence theory.[1] On a normal interpretation, the correspondence theory implies realism since it implies that there is a reality to which statements correspond if they are true; but realism does not by itself imply the correspondence theory, since it does not imply that "truth" is the name of a relation of correspondence between statements and reality.

Another misconception is to suppose that there is something epistemic about realism. Thus, for example, Hilary Putnam writes[2]

the whole content of Realism lies in the claim that it makes sense to think of a God's Eye View (or better a view from nowhere).

But that is not the content of realism as normally construed. On the contrary, the whole idea of a "view" is already epistemic and ER is not epistemic. It would be consistent with realism to suppose that any kind of "view" of reality is quite impossible. Indeed, on one interpretation, Kant's doctrine of things in themselves is a conception of a reality that is inaccessible to any "view." I realize that since the seventeenth century the most common arguments against realism have been epistemic—"all we can ever really know are our own sense data," that sort of thing—but the thesis under attack, realism, is not as it stands an epistemic thesis at all. I will have more to say later about the epistemic arguments against realism.

A third mistake, also common, is to suppose that realism is committed to the theory that there is one best vocabulary for describing reality, that reality itself must determine how it should be described. But once again, ER as defined above has no such implication. The view that the world exists independently of our representations of it does not imply that there is a privileged vocabulary for describing it. It is consistent with ER to claim the thesis of conceptual relativity (proposition 4), that different and even incommensurable vocabularies can be constructed for describing different aspects of reality for our various different purposes.

To summarize these points: realism, as I am using the term, is not a theory of truth, it is not a theory of knowledge, and it is not a theory of language. If one insists on a pigeonhole, one could say that realism is an *ontological* theory: It says that there exists a reality totally independent of our representations.

In the philosophical tradition there is a pervasive further ambiguity in the notion of realism that I need to expose and remove. Typically philosophers who discuss these issues treat them as if they concerned how the world is in fact. They think the issues between, say, realism and idealism are about the existence of matter or about objects in space and time. This is a very deep mistake. Properly understood, realism is not a thesis about how the world is in fact. We could be totally mistaken about how the world is in every detail and realism could still be true. *Realism is the view that there is a way that things are that is logically independent of all human representations. Realism does not say how things are but only that there is a way that they are.* And "things" in the previous two sentences does not mean material objects or even objects. It is, like the "it" in "It is raining," not a referring expression.

It will seem presumptuous of me to claim that the issues do not concern specific claims about matter, and about material objects in space and time, if that is in fact what the disputants thought they were arguing about. But I hope to make it clear that the issues could not be about such specific claims. Realism could not be a theory asserting the existence of Mt. Everest, for example; because if it should turn out that Mt. Everest never existed, realism remains untouched. And what goes for Mt. Everest goes for material objects in general. But what if it should turn out that material objects do not exist or even that space and time do not exist? Well, in a sense it already has turned out that way, because we now think of material objects as collections of "particles" that are not themselves material objects but are best thought of as points of mass/energy; and absolute space and time have given way to sets of relations to coordinate systems. Not only is none of this inconsistent with realism; rather, as I will argue later, it all presupposes realism. It presupposes that there is a way things are that is independent of how we represent how things are.

But let us continue with some science fiction thought experiments. Suppose it should turn out that physical reality is causally dependent on consciousness in such a way that with the last death of the last conscious agent all of physical reality blows up in a kind of Negative Big Bang. Would that still be consistent with external realism? It would, because the postulated dependence of matter on consciousness is a causal dependence like any other. When realism claims that reality exists independently of consciousness and of other forms of representation, no causal claim is made or implied. Rather, the claim is that reality is not *logically constituted* by representations, that there is no logical dependence.

"But suppose it should turn out that the only things that exist or ever did exist are states of disembodied consciousness. Surely that would be inconsistent with realism and a vindication of idealism or at least some other version of antirealism."

No, not necessarily. Realism does not say that the world had to turn out one way rather than another, but only that there is a way that it did turn out that is independent of our representations of it. Representations are one thing, the reality represented another, and this point is true even if it should turn out that the only actual reality is mental states. One way to see the difference between realism and antirealism is this: on the realist view if it turned out that only conscious states exist, then ships and shoes and sealing wax do not exist. But the claim that ships and shoes and sealing wax do not exist is a claim about external reality like any other. It presupposes realism as much as the claim that they do exist. On the antirealist view, such things, if they exist, are necessarily constituted by our representations, and they could not have existed independently of representations. For example, according to Berkeley, ships and shoes and sealing wax must be collections of states of consciousness. For the antirealist it is impossible that there should be a mind-independent reality. For the realist, even if there were no material objects in fact, there would still be a representation-independent reality, for the nonexistence of material objects would just be one feature of that representation-independent reality. The world could have been different, consistent with realism, but in fact it turned out that it contains material phenomena in space and time.

(Alternative formulation: For the realist, it not only *could have* turned out that there are objects other than representations, but in fact it *did* turn out that way. For the antirealist it could not have turned out that there are representation-independent objects.)

Strange as it may seem, realism has recently come under attack both in philosophy and in other disciplines. Thinkers as diverse as Michael Dummett, Nelson Goodman, Thomas Kuhn, Paul Feyerabend, Hilary Putnam, Richard Rorty, Jacques Derrida, Humberto Maturana, Francesco Varela, and Terry Winograd are often interpreted (not always correctly, I believe) as challenging our naive assumption that there exists a reality totally independent of our representations of it. Some scientists have even claimed that modern physics is inconsistent with realism; thus J. R. Wheeler writes,

> The universe does not exist "out there" independent of us. We
> are inescapably involved in bringing about that which ap-
> pears to be happening. We are not only observers, we are
> participators . . . in making [the] past as well as the present
> and the future.[3]

There are several disquieting things about all these attacks on realism. The first is that the arguments against our commonsense
idea that there exists an independent reality are often vague and
obscure. Sometimes no clearly stated arguments are even presented. Second, the alternative views, the views that are supposed
to be presented in opposition to realism, are often equally obscure
and unclearly stated. Even among analytic philosophers many recent discussions of realism are symptomatic of the general loose-
ness that has set in over the past couple of decades. What exactly
are the propositions being asserted? What exactly are those denied? And what exactly are the arguments for both assertion and
denial? You will look in vain for answers to these questions in most
discussions of these matters. I think, furthermore, that this general
carelessness is not accidental. It is somehow satisfying to our will
to power to think that "we" make the world, that reality itself is but
a social construct, alterable at will and subject to future changes as
"we" see fit. Equally, it seems offensive that there should be an independent reality of brute facts—blind, uncomprehending, indif-
ferent, and utterly unaffected by our concerns. And all of this is
part of the general intellectual atmosphere that makes antirealist
versions of "poststructuralism" such as deconstruction seem intel-
lectually acceptable, even exciting. But once you state the claims
and arguments of the antirealists out in the open, naked and
undisguised, they tend to look fairly ridiculous. Hence the obscu-
rity and even obscurantism of many (not all) of these discussions.

So I have a problem. I said I would defend realism against the
attacks made on it, but frankly I have trouble finding any powerful
attacks that seem worth answering. Maturana rejects the idea of
"an objective reality" in favor of the idea that nervous systems, as

autopoietic systems, construct their own reality.[4] The argument appears to be that since we have no conception of, and no access to, reality except through the social construction of realities in the "consensual domains," constructed by autopoietic systems, there is no reality existing independently of biological systems. Against this view I want to say, From the fact that our knowledge/conception/picture of reality is constructed by human brains in human interactions, it does not follow that the *reality* of which we have the knowledge/conception/picture is constructed by human brain in human interactions.* It is just a non sequitur, a genetic fallacy, to infer from the collective neurophysiological causal explanation of our knowledge of the external world to the nonexistence of the external world.

Winograd points out that the same sentence, e.g., "There is water in the refrigerator," can be used to make a false statement relative to one set of background interests, a true statement relative to another.[5] From this he concludes that reality does not exist independently of our representations. Once again, as with Maturana, the conclusion does not follow. The interest-relativity of our representations of reality does not show that the reality represented is itself interest-relative. Like Maturana, Winograd tries to derive conclusions about reality from features of our representations of reality. Several "postmodernist" literary theorists have argued that because all knowledge is socially constructed and subject to all the arbitrariness and will to power of any social construction, that therefore realism is somehow threatened. As George Levine writes, "Antirealism, even literary antirealism, depends on a sense of the impossibility of unmediated knowledge."[6] Derrida, as far as I can tell, does not have an argument. He simply declares that there is nothing outside of texts (*Il n'y a pas de "hors texte"*). And in any case, in a subsequent polemical response to

---

*There is, furthermore, a problem about the human brains and the human interactions themselves. Are they also supposed to be constructed by human interactions?

some objections of mine, he apparently takes it all back: he says that all he meant by the apparently spectacular declaration that there is nothing outside of *texts* is the banality that everything exists in some *context* or other![7] What is one to do then, in the face of an array of weak or even nonexistent arguments for a conclusion that seems preposterous?

The strategy I will follow is to take what I think are the most powerful arguments against external realism and answer them. Suppose that I were convinced by antirealism; what in particular might have convinced me? Or if that seems too farfetched, suppose the fate of humanity rested on my convincing someone else of antirealism, what arguments would I use? I will consider three arguments: the argument from *conceptual relativity,* the *verificationist* argument, and what I will call the *Ding an sich* argument.

The Argument from Conceptual Relativity Against Realism

The conceptual relativity argument is that proposition 4 above, conceptual relativity, refutes proposition 1, external realism.

The idea of conceptual relativity is an old and, I believe, a correct one. Any system of classification or individuation of objects, any set of categories for describing the world, indeed, any system of representation at all is conventional, and to that extent arbitrary. The world divides up the way we divide it, and if we are ever inclined to think that our present way of dividing it is the right one, or is somehow inevitable, we can always imagine alternative systems of classification. To illustrate this for yourself, take a piece of chalk and draw a line across a portion of the book in front of you and then onto the table and around in a circle and back to the book to connect. Now give a name to this new sort of object made of portions of surfaces of books plus tables delimited by a chalk line. Call this object a "klurg." We do not have a use for this concept in our language. But it would be easy to imagine a culture where klurgs are of great religious significance, where they can be delineated only by sacred virgins working under water and their obliteration merits the death penalty. But if "klurg" is a new concept with previously unheard-of truth conditions, there is no limit to how many new concepts we can form. Because any true description of the world will always be made within some vocabulary, some system of concepts, conceptual relativity has the consequence that any true description is always made relative to some system of concepts that we have more or less arbitrarily selected for describing the world.

So characterized, conceptual relativism seems completely true, indeed, platitudinous. However, several philosophers have supposed that it is inconsistent with external realism, and consequently, that if we accept conceptual relativism, we are forced to deny realism. But if this claim were really true, we ought to be able to state the two theses precisely enough for the inconsistency to be quite obvious.

Let external realism be the view that:

ER1: Reality exists independently of our representations of it.

Let the relevant thesis of conceptual relativism be the view that:

CR1: All representations of reality are made relative to some more or less arbitrarily selected set of concepts.

So stated, these two views do not even have the *appearance* of inconsistency. The first just says that there is something out there to be described. The second says that we have to select a set of concepts and a vocabulary to describe it. So why would anyone suppose that the second entails the negation of the first? The answer is that if we accept conceptual relativism, and try to conjoin it with realism, we appear to get inconsistencies.

Consider the following example from Putnam.[8] Imagine that there is some part of the world as shown in Figure 7.1.

How many objects are there in this miniworld? Well, according to Carnap's system of arithmetic (and according to common

Figure 7.1

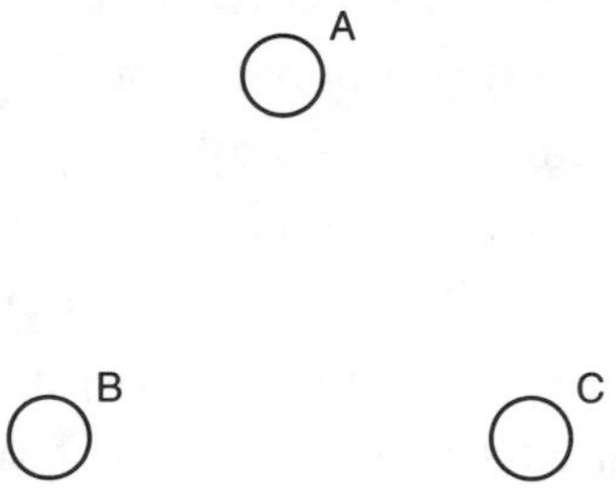

sense), there are three; but according to Lesniewski and other Polish logicians, there are seven objects in this world, counted as follows:

$$1 = A$$
$$2 = B$$
$$3 = C$$
$$4 = A + B$$
$$5 = A + C$$
$$6 = B + C$$
$$7 = A + B + C$$

So how many objects are there really in the imagined world? Are there really three or really seven? There is no absolute answer to these questions. The only answers we can give are relative to the arbitrary choice of conceptual schemes. The same sentence, e.g., "There are exactly three objects in the world," will be true in one scheme, false in the other. The heart of the argument is that external realism leads to inconsistencies because it allows for inconsistent descriptions of the supposedly independently existing reality.

The form in which the argument occurs in Goodman is that we characteristically make reality or, as Goodman would prefer to say, we "make worlds" by drawing certain boundaries rather than others. For example, Goodman says,

Now as we thus make constellations by picking out and putting together certain stars rather than others, so we make stars by drawing certain boundaries rather than others. Nothing dictates whether the sky shall be marked off into constellations or other objects, we have to make what we find, be it the Great Dipper, Sirius, food, fuel, or a stereo system.[9]

Goodman rejects realism and evades the inconsistencies by relativizing the facts described to a "world" that we make. Putnam says that instead of thinking that there is a mind-independent reality, we should say rather that "the mind and the world jointly make up the mind and the world."[10]

But are these supposed contradictions really a problem? About the miniworld example, a realist who was a convinced conceptual relativist would say that there really are three objects, as the criterion for counting objects has been set in the first system of classification, really seven as the criterion has been set in the second. And this answer removes the apparent contradiction, not by modifying or abandoning external realism but by simply pointing out that the criterion for counting objects has been set in two different ways. Thus the same sentence, e.g., "There are exactly three objects in the world," can now be used to make two quite different and independent statements, one of which is true, one false. But the real world does not care how we describe it and it remains the same under the various different descriptions we give of it.

Some of the examples of conceptual relativism given in the literature are more arcane and complicated than the ones I have given, but the principle they employ is the same, and I cannot see that anything is gained by the complexity. They all are designed to show that different conceptual systems will generate different and apparently inconsistent descriptions of the same "reality." As far as I can see there is nothing in any of them that is inconsistent with external realism. The appearance of inconsistency is an illusion and, on a natural interpretation of these views, there is no inconsistency whatever in accepting the most naive version of realism, and accepting any version at all of conceptual relativism.*

Think of the relation of realism and conceptual relativism like this: Take a corner of the world, say, the Himalayas, and think of it as it was prior to the existence of any human beings. Now imagine that humans come along and represent the facts in various different ways. They have different vocabularies, different systems for making maps, different ways of counting one mountain, two mountains, the same mountain, etc. Next, imagine that eventually the humans all cease to exist. Now what happens to the existence of the Himalayas and all the facts about the Himalayas in the course of these vicissitudes? Absolutely nothing. Different descriptions of facts, objects, etc., came and went, but the facts, objects, etc., remained unaffected. (Does anyone really doubt this?)

---

*What has gone wrong? In Putnam's case a close look at the texts suggests that he is lumping at least two logically independent theses under his label, "Metaphysical Realism."

First: Reality exists independently of our representations of it.

Second: There is one and only one correct conceptual scheme for describing reality.

The first is what I have been calling external realism; let's call the second the theory of the "Privileged Conceptual Scheme" (PCS). Putnam sees correctly that CR refutes PCS. And since you can always refute a conjunction by refuting one conjunct, if metaphysical realism is the conjunction of ER and PCS, then metaphysical realism has been refuted. But you do not refute both conjuncts by refuting just one; so the falsity of PCS leaves ER standing untouched. Putnam's writings give the impression that he thinks that by refuting PCS he has refuted ER. Perhaps he does not think that the "refutation" touches ER, in which case a bald assertion in favor of ER would have been helpful to his readers. But he makes no such assertion; on the contrary, he endorses a view he calls "internal realism." I do not think there is a coherent position of "internal realism" that is halfway between external realism, as I have defined it, and out-and-out antirealism, which Putnam also claims to reject.

The fact that alternative conceptual schemes allow for different descriptions of the same reality, and that there are no descriptions of reality outside all conceptual schemes, has no bearing whatever on the truth of realism.

But what about the possibility, raised by Goodman, of inconsistent descriptions made relative to different conceptual schemes? There is no substitute for going carefully through examples, so let us consider a case of how external realism deals with alternative vocabularies. Let us suppose that I am a complete, naive external realist where weight, i.e., the gravitational attraction of masses at the earth's surface, is concerned. I think that I really weigh 160 no matter what anybody thinks. But wait! I weigh 160 in pounds but only 73 in kilograms. So how much do I weigh really: 160 or 73? I hope it is obvious that both answers are correct, though each is incomplete. The appearance of inconsistency is only an appearance, because the claim that I weigh 160 in pounds is consistent with the claim that I weigh 73 in kilograms. External realism allows for an infinite number of true descriptions of the same reality made relative to different conceptual schemes. "What is my aim in philosophy? To teach you to turn disguised nonsense into obvious nonsense."[11] It is disguised nonsense to say that conceptual relativism implies antirealism, obvious nonsense to say that I cannot, at the same time, weigh both 160 (in pounds) and 73 (in kilograms).

Furthermore, if conceptual relativity is to be used as an argument against realism, it seems to presuppose realism, because it presupposes a language-independent reality that can be carved up or divided up in different ways, by different vocabularies. Think of the example of alternative arithmetics: Putnam points out that one way to describe the miniworld is to say there are three objects, another way is to say there are seven objects. But notice that this very claim presupposes something there to be described prior to the application of the description; otherwise there is no way we could even understand the example. And when Goodman writes, "We make stars by drawing certain boundaries

rather than others," there is no way to understand that claim except by presupposing something there on which we can draw
boundaries. Unless there is already a territory on which we can
draw boundaries, there is no possibility of drawing any boundaries.

If we try to take these arguments as counting against ER, we
commit a massive use-mention fallacy: From the fact that a *description* can only be made relative to a set of linguistic categories,
it does not follow that the *facts/objects/states of affairs,/etc., described* can only *exist* relative to a set of categories. Conceptual
relativism, properly understood, is an account of how we fix the
application of our terms: What counts as a correct application of
the term "cat" or "kilogram" or "canyon" (or "klurg") is up to us to
decide and is to that extent arbitrary. *But once we have fixed the
meaning of such terms in our vocabulary by arbitrary definitions, it
is no longer a matter of any kind of relativism or arbitrariness
whether representation-independent features of the world satisfy
those definitions, because the features of the world that satisfy or
fail to satisfy the definitions exist independently of those or any
other definitions.* We arbitrarily define the word "cat" in such and
such a way; and only relative to such and such definitions can we
say, "That's a cat." But once we have made the definitions and
once we have applied the concepts relative to the system of definitions, whether or not something satisfies our definition is no
longer arbitrary or relative. That we use the word "cat" the way we
do is up to us; that there is an object that exists independently of
that use, and satisfies that use, is a plain matter of (absolute, intrinsic, mind-independent) fact. Contrary to Goodman, we do not
make "worlds"; we make *descriptions* that the actual world may fit
or fail to fit. But all this implies that there is a reality that exists independently of our system of concepts. Without such a reality,
there is nothing to apply the concept to.

In order that we should get a version of conceptual relativism
that is inconsistent with external realism, we would have to have a
version that implies that the same statement (not the same sen-

tence, but the same statement) could be true of the world in one conceptual system but false of the world in another conceptual system. I have not seen any example of this that is remotely plausible. The standard examples are something like this: Assume that we have different models for representing some domain of reality, say, Aristotelian physics vs. Newtonian physics or the Mercator projection of the earth's surface vs. a standard globe representation of the earth's surface. Now, on the Mercator projection, Greenland occupies a bigger area than Brazil, but on the globe, Greenland occupies a smaller area than Brazil. So don't we have here two models, both true of the same reality, but, in fact, inconsistent with each other? The answer is no. The Mercator projection is just inaccurate about the relative size of Brazil and Greenland. It is a well-known fact that certain models, e.g., Aristotelian physics and the Mercator projection, are mistaken about or distort certain features of the world.

All true statements about the world can consistently be affirmed together. Indeed, if they could not consistently be affirmed together, they could not all be true. Of course, we are always confronted with the problems of vagueness, indeterminacy, family resemblance, open texture, contextual dependency, the incommensurability of theories, ambiguity, the idealization involved in theory construction, alternative interpretations, the underdetermination of theory by evidence, and all the rest of it. But these are features of our systems of representation, not of the representation-independent reality that some of these systems can be used, more less adequately, to represent. Often the same sentence can be used to assert a truth in one conceptual scheme and a falsehood in another conceptual scheme. But this, as we have seen over and over, does not show a genuine inconsistency.

The Verificationist Argument

Twentieth-century philosophy has been obsessed with language and meaning, and that is why it is perhaps inevitable that somebody would come up with the idea that nothing at all exists apart from language and meaning. Earlier centuries were obsessed with experience and knowledge, and correspondingly philosophers came up with the idea that there is no reality independent of experience and knowledge. In the history of Western philosophy since the seventeenth century, the most common argument against realism has been derived from epistemic considerations.

I believe the basic philosophical motivation behind verificationists' arguments against realism is to try to eliminate the possibility of skepticism by removing the gulf between appearance and reality that makes skepticism possible in the first place. If reality consists in nothing but our experiences, if our experiences are somehow constitutive of reality, then the form of skepticism that says we can never get out of our experiences to the reality beyond is answered.

This is a persistent urge in philosophy. Kant's transcendental idealism is a more sophisticated variant of it than one finds in Berkeley, and the same urge survives in the late twentieth century in the various efforts to analyze meaning in "public" terms, or even "behavioristically," so that there will be no private residue about which one might doubt that one had really understood what other people meant by the use of an expression.

Even if I am right about this diagnosis, however, it doesn't answer the actual arguments, so I will now present what I take to be the most powerful verificationists' argument against realism: Here is how it goes:

Ask yourself what you really know, I mean *really* know. Well, you might say you really know that you are sitting on a chair, that there is a desk in front of you, that you are looking at a computer screen. But if you think about it, you will see that what you really know is that you are having certain experiences; so when you make these claims about a chair or a desk or a computer screen, either you are talking about your experiences or you are talking about something you don't really know. Furthermore, if you tried to talk about something other than experiences you would be talking about something that you couldn't know. If you ask how you know about the world, the answer has to be: from your experiences. But then you are faced with a dilemma. Either your claims to know simply report the content of your experiences or they go beyond those contents. If the former, then there is nothing known except the content of your experiences. If the latter, then you are making claims that you cannot validate, because all validation rests on experience, and you are ex hypothesi making claims that go beyond what you experience.

For example, I claim to know there is a desk in front of me now. What does such a claim mean? Well, all I have direct knowledge of are these tactile and visual experiences, and all I—or anyone else—could ever have direct knowledge of are more such experiences. So what does my original claim amount to? Either it amounts to the claim that there are actual and possible experiences ("sense data" in the twentieth-century jargon, "ideas" and "impressions" in that of the seventeenth and eighteenth centuries), or if something more is claimed, then it must be a claim about something totally unknowable and inaccessible to any investigation. Such a claim is empirically empty. The conclusion is obvious: experience is constitutive of reality.

This argument occurs in several authors and the conclusion has been stated in a variety of vocabularies: Objects are collections of ideas (Berkeley). Objects are permanent possibilities of sensation (Mill). Empirical statements can be translated without residue into statements about sense data (twentieth-century phenomenalism). Berkeley summarizes this argument neatly when he says, "If matter did exist we could never know it, if it does not exist everything remains the same."

There are, it seems to me, two strands to the argument. The first is, all we can ever perceive are our own experiences. Therefore, if there is supposed to be a reality beyond our experiences, it is unknowable, and ultimately unintelligible. The second is an extension of the first. It says the only basis we have for claims about the real world are our experiences. Therefore, if claims about the real world go beyond the content of our experiences, then ex hypothesi we are postulating something for which we can have no epistemic basis.

I believe both strands are mistaken. Let us consider each in turn. It is indeed the case that whenever one consciously perceives anything, one has certain experiences. For example, for every visual perception there is a corresponding visual experience. In the formal mode of speech, to report "I see the table" implies "I am having a certain sort of visual experience." But from the fact that the visual experience is an essential component of the visual perception, it does not follow that the visual experience is that which is perceived. It does not follow, in short, that one does not have direct access to the real world whenever one employs one's perceptual apparatus to perceive it. Thus, for example, right now I see my desk in front of me. In such a case, I simply perceive the desk. In so doing, I have a perceptual experience, but the perceptual experience is neither the object of perception nor is it the evidence on the basis of which I conclude that there is a desk there. I do not "conclude" on the basis of "evidence" that there is a desk here; rather, I simply see it. So the first strand in the argument, namely, that all we have access to in perceptual experiences is the content of the perception itself, is mistaken.[12]

I believe that the second is also mistaken. Let us grant, for the sake of argument, that the epistemic basis for my present claim that there is a desk in front of me is the existence of my present sense experiences and grant also that the claim that there is a table there—if it is understood in the commonsense, naive realist way—states more than a mere summary of statements about my experiences. What follows? Does it follow that the claim that there is a table there states something unknowable, something that goes beyond any possible evidence or other epistemic basis? It does not follow. From the fact that the epistemic basis for my knowledge is my present experiences, it does not follow that all I can know are my experiences. On the contrary, the way we described the example was precisely as a case where my experiences give me access to something that is not itself an experience.

It is a familiar point in philosophy that in general empirical claims go beyond the epistemic bases on which they are made. There would not be much point, for example, in making scientific hypotheses if they were just summaries of the available evidence.

However, at this point, the defender of the antirealist position will want to say the following:

In presenting these answers to the antirealist argument, you have tacitly presupposed that you are really perceiving mind-independent objects in the real world, but that is precisely what you are not entitled to assume. The whole point of the argument is that you could be having exactly these experiences and there not be any desk there. But if that is the case, then it doesn't matter whether we think of the experiences as providing the "evidence" for your "conclusion" that there is a desk there. The point is that the only basis that you have for your confidence that there is a desk there is the presence of these sense data, and if the desk is supposed to be something over and above the sense data, they would not be sufficient to justify that confidence because you could be having exactly these experiences and be totally mistaken. The postulation of an external reality is essentially the postulation of something unknowable and ultimately unintelligible.

What is the answer to this? In this discussion I am not trying to answer general skepticism. That is a set of questions that goes beyond the scope of this book. So for the sake of this argument let us just grant that I might be having exactly these experiential contents and be having a total hallucination. I might be subject to all the horrors of traditional epistemology: I might be a brain in a vat,

I might be deceived by an evil demon, I might be dreaming, etc. But it does not follow that my claim that there is a desk in front of me is simply a summary of the experiences that prompt me to make the claim. That is, even if skepticism is right, and I am systematically mistaken, *what I am mistaken about are the features of the real world.* The possibility of being systematically mistaken about those features does not show that my claims about them are just summaries of statements about my sense experiences.

These are ancient battlegrounds, and the landscape is much devastated by epistemic wars, but I believe the basic logical geography of the philosophical terrain is simple and readily discernible: The verificationist argument for antirealism is as follows:

1. All we have access to in perception are the contents of our own experiences.

2. The only epistemic basis we can have for claims about the external world are our perceptual experiences.

Therefore,

3. The only reality we can meaningfully speak of is the reality of perceptual experiences.

I have argued that statement 1 is false. We typically perceive objects and states of affairs in the world. Furthermore, I have argued that statement 2, though true, does not imply statement 3. It is a mistake to suppose that empirical claims are only meaningful to the extent that they are understood as summaries of their evidentiary or epistemic bases. Finally, I have claimed that the possibility of radical error, the possibility raised by skepticism, is irrelevant. Even if we are systematically mistaken, à la traditional skepticism, statement 3 does not follow. On the contrary, what we are mistaken about, if skepticism is right, is the real world.

I realize that there are other versions of the verificationists' argument for antirealism, but I believe this version has been the most pervasive in the empiricist tradition from the seventeenth century right through logical positivism. I also realize that in this entire tradition epistemology, in general, and the attempt to answer Cartesian skepticism, in particular, were central to the entire philosophical enterprise. I regard these as mistakes. Epistemology has an important but certainly not a central place in the enterprise of philosophy. The deeper reason why epistemological considerations of the sort that I have been discussing could never provide a sound argument for antirealism is that in order even to state these considerations, we have to presuppose realism. I will return to this point in the next chapter.

The *Ding an Sich* Argument

There is another argument against ER worth mentioning, the argument concerning things in themselves, the *Ding an sich* argument.

It is hard to find an explicit version of this argument in contemporary philosophy, but it keeps coming up in the oral tradition. It is best to think of it as a combination of the argument from conceptual relativity and the argument from verification. Here is how it goes:

When we deal with the world in perception, thought, inquiry, etc., we are always working from within some conceptual scheme. Even our so-called "experiences" are never directly of "reality" but are permeated by our concepts, and can refer ultimately only to other experiences. There is no God's-eye view from which we can survey the relations between our representations and the reality they are alleged to represent, to see whether they are really adequate to reality. There is no way we can see these relations from the side; rather, we are always inside our representations—our beliefs, experiences, utterances, etc. Because we can't get outside the set of our representations to scrutinize reality directly, because there is no nonrepresentational standpoint from which we can survey the relations between representation and reality, and because there is not even the possibility of assessing the adequacy of our representations by measuring them against things in themselves, talk of a transcendent reality must be just so much nonsense. All the reality we can ever really get at, have access to, is the reality that is internal to our system of representations. Within the system there is a possibility of realism, internal realism, but the idea of a reality outside the system is as empty as Kant's notion of the *Ding on sich*, a thing in itself, beyond the grasp not only of our knowledge but of our language and thought. What external realism offers us is an unthinkable something, indescribable, inaccessible, unknowable, unspeakable, and ultimately nonsensical. The real problem with such a realism is not that it is false, but that it is ultimately unintelligible.

What are we to make of this argument? Once again, if we try to state it as an explicit argument, with a set of premises and a conclusion, it is hard to see how the conclusion is supposed to follow.

Premise: Any cognitive state occurs as part of a set of cognitive states and within a cognitive system.

From this premise it is supposed to follow that:

Conclusion 1: It is impossible to get outside of all cognitive states and systems to survey the relationships between them and the reality that they are used to cognize.

And from this in turn it is supposed to follow that:

Conclusion 2: No cognition is ever of a reality that exists independently of cognition.

It seems to me that, properly understood, conclusion 1 does indeed follow from the premise. All representation occurs within a set of representations and within some representational system.

Hence, any representation of the relation between the set of representational states and the representational system, on the one hand, and the reality represented, on the other, also occurs within some representational system. But so what? It simply does not follow from the fact that all cognition is within a cognitive system that no cognition is ever directly of a reality that exists independently of all cognition. Conclusion 2 just does not follow. Indeed, to suppose it does follow seems to be a mistake of the same form as the mistake committed by old-time idealism.

Diagnosis of the Problem

I now want to offer a partial diagnosis of why it has become fashionable even among technically competent philosophers to attack realism, and to advance such feeble arguments against it.

One of the oldest urges in Western philosophy is to think that somehow or other truth and reality should coincide. That somehow or other, if there really were such things as truth and reality, as we normally think of them, then truth would have to provide an exact mirror of reality. The nature of reality itself would have to provide the exact structure of true statements. A classical statement of this position is in Wittgenstein's *Tractatus*,[13] but I believe the idea is as old as Plato. When the philosopher despairs of achieving an exact isomorphism between the structure of reality and the structure of true representations, the temptation is to think that somehow or other our naive notions of truth and reality have been discredited. But they have not been discredited. What has been discredited is a certain misconception of the relationship between truth and reality.

There is a simple but deep reason why truth and reality cannot coincide in a way that many philosophers think that the naive external realist is committed to their coincidence. The reason is this: All representation, and a fortiori all truthful representation, is always under certain aspects and not others. The aspectual character of all representations derives from such facts as that representation is always made from within a certain conceptual scheme and from a certain point of view. So, for example, if I describe the substance in front of me as water, the same piece of reality is represented as if I describe it as H_2O. But, of course, I am representing the same stuff under a different aspect if I represent it as water than if I represent it as H_2O. Strictly speaking, there is an indefinitely large number of different points of view, different aspects, and different conceptual systems under which anything can be represented. If that is right, and it surely is, then it will be impossible to get the coincidence between truth and reality after which so many traditional philosophers seem to hanker. Every representation has an aspectual shape. It represents its target under certain aspects and not others. In short, it is only from a point of view that we represent reality, but ontologically objective reality does not have a point of view.

Does the Real World Exist?

Part II: Could There Be a Proof of External Realism?

Realism as a Background Condition
of Intelligibility

I have said that certain standard arguments against realism are
invalid. Are there any arguments to be given in its favor? There is
something puzzling about demanding an argument to show that
the world exists independently of our representations of it. I realize that Kant thought it a scandal that there was no such proof,
and Moore thought he could give proof just by holding up his two
hands. But, one feels, in the way that Kant posed his demand
nothing could have satisfied it, and Moore's attempt to satisfy it
somehow "misses the point." Yet, at the same time, one feels that
one ought to satisfy Kant's demand, and that at some level Moore
was surely right. He certainly did have two hands, and if he had
two hands then the external world exists. Right? What is going on?

We need to explain both our urge to prove external realism and our sense that any proof begs the question.

The demand for a proof of external realism is a bit like the demands one used to hear in the 1960s for a proof of rationality—"What is your argument for rationality?"—in that the very posing of the challenge somehow presupposes what is challenged. Any attempt to provide an "argument" or "proof" already presupposes standards of rationality, because the applicability of those standards is constitutive of something's being an argument or proof. In a word, you can't prove rationality by argument because arguments already presuppose rationality. There are a number of such general frameworks where the demand to justify the framework from within the framework is always senseless and yet somehow seems incumbent upon us. Thus, although one can prove that a particular argument is valid or rational within the criteria of rationality and validity, one cannot prove within those criteria that rationality is rational or that validity is valid. Similarly, one can establish that a given sequence of words is a grammatical or ungrammatical English sentence, but one cannot establish that English as a language is grammatical or ungrammatical, because English sets the standard for grammaticality in English. The effort to establish external realism by some sort of "argument" would be analogous to one of these efforts. It would be as if one tried to establish that representation represents. One can show that this or that claim corresponds or fails to correspond to how things really are in the "external world," but one cannot in that way show that the claim that there is an external world corresponds to how things are in the external world, because any question of corresponding or failing to correspond to the external world already presupposes the existence of an external world to which the claim corresponds or fails to correspond. External realism is thus not a thesis nor an hypothesis but the condition of having certain sorts of theses or hypotheses.

You can see that something is wrong with this entire debate if you look at standard contemporary arguments in favor of external realism. A standard argument, perhaps the standard argument, for realism is that convergence in science provides a kind of empirical proof of realism. The idea is that because different scientific investigators working at different times and places come up with the same or similar results, the best explanation for their doing so is that there is an independently existing reality that causes them to converge on the same hypotheses and theories. The difficulty with this argument is that in our understanding of the possibility of there being such phenomena as either convergence or failure of convergence, we are already presupposing realism. In order for us even to raise the question whether scientific investigation does converge in the suggested fashion, we have to presuppose an independently existing reality of investigators engaging in investigations. These investigations either converge or fail to converge; that is, the entire discussion of convergence presupposes realism, because it presupposes that the statement "Science converges," whether true or false, concerns a reality independent of that or any other statement. Another way to put this point: In areas where science fails to converge, e.g., social psychology, our recognition of the failure provides exactly as much *evidence* for realism as our recognition of those areas in which it does converge, i.e., it provides no *evidence* at all, since in recognizing something as either convergence or nonconvergence, we are already taking realism for granted.

I realize that the convergence argument is often presented as an argument for the existence of unobservable entities postulated by scientific theories and not as a general argument for external realism. But then it is faced with a dilemma. If, on the one hand, the convergence argument is an argument to establish the existence of this or that type of unobservable entity, say, electrons, then the notion of convergence adds nothing whatever to the usual notions of evidence, verification, and truth. If the atomic theory that postulates electrons is confirmed in both my lab and yours, then that is further evidence that the theory is true, and if the theory entails that electrons exist, then we have good evidence that electrons exist. The notion of convergence adds nothing to this story. And the fact that we may have a number of such stories about different types of unobservable entities still gives us nothing more than a list of cases of scientific confirmation and disconfirmation. But if, on the other hand, the convergence argument is to be a genuine metatheory about the sociology of scientific research, a theory to the effect that, as a matter of second-order empirical fact, scientists working at different times and places tend to produce convergent results, results that agree from one lab to another, and that this convergence is confirming evidence for realism, then it is subject to the objection I made earlier: In order that we can even consider the problem of convergence we have to presuppose realism.

To explore this point further I want to ask, what is wrong with Moore's "proof"? Moore thought that by proving the existence of two or more things such as hands, sheets of paper, shoes, socks, etc., he would have proven the existence of "things outside of us" and ipso facto would have proven the existence of an "External World," because, as he says, "it will follow at once that there are some things to be met with in space."* On this view the relation between his premise and conclusion is a straight entailment relation: The proposition that I have two hands entails the proposition that the external world exists. The existence of the external world is a truth condition of the proposition that I have two hands in the same way that the existence of at least one hand is a truth condition of that proposition. If I have two hands then it fol-

---

*The crucial passage is this:

That is to say, if I can prove that there exist now both a sheet of paper and a human hand, I shall have proved that there are now 'things outside of us'; if I can prove that there exist now both a shoe and sock, I shall have proved that there are now 'things outside of us'; etc.; and similarly I shall have proved it, if I can prove that there exist now two sheets of paper, or two human hands, or two shoes, or two socks, etc. Obviously, then, there are thousands of different things such that, if, at any time, I can prove any one of them, I shall have proved the existence of things outside of us. Cannot I prove any of these things?

It seems to me that, so far from its being true, as Kant declares to be his opinion, that there is only one possible proof of the existence of things outside of us,

lows immediately that "there are things to be met with in space." And he establishes the "premise" by demonstration. He simply makes a certain gesture and thereby "proves" the existence of his hands. But there is something fishy about this. Berkeley, for example, would have agreed that Moore had two hands but would have challenged the alleged entailment, so it looks as if Moore is "begging the question." Isn't the entailment precisely what is at issue?

I suggest that there are at least two worrisome features of Moore's proof: The first is the assumption that ER is a truth condition like any other, and the second is the related assumption that realism is a theory about external "objects" in "space." Against these views, the claims I want to make are: First, though there is no sharp dividing line between the two, we need to make a general distinction between truth conditions and conditions on intelligibility. There are conditions on the intelligibility of discourse, and indeed on the functioning of intentionality in general, that are not like paradigmatic cases of truth conditions. In the normal understanding of discourse we take these conditions for granted; and unless we took them for granted, we could not understand utterances the way we do or even have the intentional states with conditions of satisfaction that we have. In earlier writings I divided some of these conditions into a Network of beliefs and other intentional states, on the one hand, and a Background of abilities, capacities, etc., on the other. The claim I make here is that ER

---

namely the one which he has given, I can now give a large number of different proofs, each of which is a perfectly rigorous proof; and that at many other times I have been in a position to give many others. I can prove now, for instance, that two human hands exist. How? By holding up my two hands, and saying, as I make a certain gesture with the right hand, 'here is one hand', and adding, as I make a certain gesture with the left, 'and here is another'. And if, by doing this, I have proved *ipso facto* the existence of external things, you will all see that I can also do it now in numbers of other ways: there is no need to multiply examples. G. E. Moore, Philosophical Papers, "Proof of an External World" (London: George Allen & Unwin, 1959), pp. 145–46.

functions as a taken-for-granted part of the Background. Unless we take ER for granted, we cannot understand utterances the way we normally do. Furthermore we have to take ER for granted to engage in the sorts of discourse and thought that we have been engaging in. The presupposition of ER is thus a *necessary* presupposition for a large chunk of thought and language. We can't give it up as, for example, centuries ago we gave up our presupposition that the earth is flat.

And the second response I want to make to Moore is that once we see that ER so construed is not an empirical thesis but rather a condition of intelligibility on having certain sorts of theses, then we can see that it has no special connection to the theory that there are "objects" in "space." As I said at the beginning of Chapter 7, even if it should turn out that our notions of "objects" and "space" have to be radically revised, as in fact they have been revised by atomic theory and relativity theory, all the same, ER remains untouched. Carefully stated, external realism is the thesis that there is a way that things are that is independent of all representations of how things are.

The thesis that there is a reality independent of our representations identifies not how things are in fact, but rather identifies *a space of possibilities.* Using a Wittgensteinian style of example, we can think of it this way. Suppose I say, "I have no money at all in my wallet." Now that utterance does not logically imply the existence of money. You cannot infer from

$$\sim(\exists x) \text{ (money } x \text{ \& in my wallet } x)$$

(It is not the case that there is some x such that x is money and x is in my wallet.)

to

$$(\exists x) \text{ (money } x)$$

(There is some x such that x is money.)

But all the same the original utterance only makes the kind of sense it does, we only understand it the way we do, against the presupposition of the existence of money. It has its sense against a space of possibilities of having money. In that sense, External Realism articulates a space of possibilities for a very large number of statements.

A "Transcendental" Argument for External Realism.

If these suggestions—that ER is a Background presupposition and not an empirical theory, and that it is purely formal without any specific content about, for example, objects in space—are right, the only argument we could give for ER would be a "transcendental" argument in one of Kant's many senses of that term: We assume that a certain condition holds, and then try to show the presuppositions of that condition.

In order to do this, however, we have to make precise what the view is that we are arguing against. Antirealism is not a single doctrine but comes in different versions. For this discussion, the two most important are, first, the view that all reality consists in conscious states, and, second, the view that reality is socially constructed, that what we think of as "the real world" is just a bunch of things constructed by groups of people. To have labels, let us call the first view "phenomenalist idealism," and the second "social constructionism."

There is a simple transcendental argument against phenomenalist idealism. I said that a transcendental argument is one that assumes a certain condition obtains and then tries to show the presuppositions of that condition. In this case, however, the "condition" has to do with our practices and the "presupposition" is what we, from our own first-person point of view, must presuppose when we engage in those practices. The condition is that we do in fact attempt to communicate with each other by making certain sorts of utterances in a public language and the presupposition is external realism. To spell this out a little bit more precisely: the assumption we are making is that there is a normal way of understanding utterances, and that when performing speech acts in a public language, speakers typically attempt to achieve normal understanding. The point we are attempting to show is that for a large class (to be specified further) a condition of intelligibility for the normal understanding of these utterances is that there is a way that things are that is independent of human representations. The consequence is that *when we attempt to communicate to achieve normal understanding with these sorts of utterances we must presuppose external realism.*

Notice that we are not trying to prove the truth of external realism. I do not believe there could be a non-question-begging argument for ER. But we can show that when we engage in certain sorts of talk we presuppose external realism.

To develop the argument I need to explain the notion of "normal understanding." For most speech acts there is a commonsense or normal understanding. Often this is given by disquotation; for example, the normal understanding of the utterance "I have two hands" is that it asserts that the speaker has two hands. But wherever there is disquotation there must always be further ways of describing normal understanding. Thus in the normal understanding of "I have two hands," for example, there must be a possible description of what a hand is.

If you follow out the line of describing normal understanding, you soon reach conditions that are not truth conditions, at least not as usually construed. To see this, ask yourself what sorts of things we automatically take for granted when we understand Moore's claim, "I have two hands." As we saw in Chapter 6, there are lots of features of the Background that are not explicit in the semantic content of the sentence but that we automatically take for granted. For example, we take it for granted that Moore's hands stand in a certain relation to the rest of his body. We would understand the sentence quite differently if we understood it on analogy with the following: "I have two diamond necklaces and I keep them both in a bank vault in Switzerland and I have two hands and I keep them in the same bank vault."

But where in the sentence does it say or imply that Moore's hands are not to be kept in a bank vault or even that they are attached to his body? This is one of the things that we simply take for granted. There is no limit to the number of such Background and Network presuppositions that we have to make in order to understand even such a simple utterance as Moore's. Thus, for example, suppose that we took it for granted that if Moore has two hands, they are attached to his body all right, but they are growing out of his left ear. Or perhaps that they are attached to his arms, but his body has shrunk to the size of a grain of sand, and his two hands have grown to be each as big as the Atlantic Ocean. Again, suppose we assumed that if people have hands, they flash in and out of existence like an intermittent flashlight beam. With such crazy alterations in the Background, we would understand the sentence quite differently from the way we currently understand it. The point is that in our normal understanding we take a great deal for granted, but many of these conditions on our normal understanding cannot be thought of as truth conditions on the utterance without considerable distortion. These are the sorts of conditions that help us to *fix* the truth conditions of our utterances. They are not themselves part of those truth conditions.

The claim I now want to substantiate is, External Realism is a Background presupposition on the normal understanding of a very large class of utterances. But it differs from many other Background presuppositions in that it is both pervasive and essential. It is pervasive in the sense that it applies to a very large class of utterances; it is essential in the sense that we cannot preserve normal understanding of these utterances without it. To see that it is pervasive, notice that it applies to a large range of quite different kinds of utterances such as

Mt. Everest has snow and ice near the summit.
My dog has fleas.
Hydrogen atoms each contain one electron.

To show that it is *essential* we need to remind ourselves that the sentences in question, as sentences of a *public* language, are assumed to be understood in the *same* way by any competent speaker and hearer. Normal understanding requires sameness of understanding by both speaker and hearer, and sameness of understanding in these cases requires that utterances of the referring expressions purport to make reference to a *publicly* accessible reality, to a reality that is ontologically objective. But the condition on public accessibility to the sorts of phenomena in these examples is that the way that things are does not depend on your or my representations. You and I can both understand the utterances above—about Mt. Everest, my dog, and hydrogen atoms—in the same way, because we take it for granted that the utterances are about a publicly accessible reality. And this point holds even if the particular references fail because of the nonexistence of the entities we are trying to refer to. Even if turns out that Mt. Everest and hydrogen atoms had never existed, and I never had a dog, all the same, we still understand the utterances as depending for their normal intelligibility on the existence of an external reality. We almost want to say, "Even if no Mt. Everest, no hydrogen atoms and no Searle dog, all the same *External Reality would still be such that:* no Everest, no hydrogen atoms and no dog." But that is the wrong way to say it, because it makes it look as if each utterance contains a concealed reference to some special entity called "External Reality" with capital E and R; and that is precisely what we do not want to say. What we should say, rather, is this: A public language presupposes a public world in the sense that many (not all) utterances of a public language purport to make references to phenomena that are ontologically objective, and they ascribe such and such features to these phenomena. Now, in order that we should understand these utterances as having these truth conditions—the existence of these phenomena and the possession of these features—we have to take for granted that there is a way that the world is that is independent of our representations. But that requirement is precisely the requirement of external realism. And the consequence of this point for the present discussion is that efforts to communicate in a public language require that we presuppose a public world. And the sense of "public" in question requires that the public reality exists independently of *representations* of that reality.

The point is *not* that in understanding the utterance we have to presuppose the existence of specific objects of reference, such as Mt. Everest, hydrogen atoms, or dogs. No, the conditions of intelligibility are still preserved even if it should turn out that none of these ever existed. The existence of Mt. Everest is one of the truth conditions of the statement; but the existence of a way that things are in the world independently of our representations of them is not a truth condition but rather a condition of the form of intelligibility that such statements have.

The point is not epistemic. It is about conditions of intelligibility and not conditions of knowledge, because the point applies whether or not our statements are known or unknown, and whether they are true or false, and even whether the objects purportedly referred to exist or not. The point is simply that when we understand an utterance of the sorts we have been considering, we understand it as presupposing a publicly accessible reality.

There is another way to work up to the same conclusion. Any truth claim presupposes that there is a way that things are regarding the content of that claim. And this point holds as much for mathematical statements such as

$$2 + 2 = 4$$

or for statements about personal experiences such as

I am in pain

as it does for statements about mountains, dogs, and electrons. What is special about these latter sorts of statements is that they purport to make reference to publicly accessible phenomena, in these examples, publicly accessible physical objects. But for such cases we presuppose not only that there is a way that things are that is independent of our representations, but that *there is a way that things are in a publicly accessible, i.e., ontologically objective, realm.* But the presupposition of a mind-independent reality already contains the presupposition of a representation-independent reality, and that presupposition just is external realism. ER, so construed, is a purely formal constraint. It does not say how things are but only that there is a way that they are that is independent of our representations. The argument so far can be summarized in a series of steps:

1. The normal understanding of utterances in a public language requires that the utterances be understandable in *the same way* by any competent speaker and hearer of the language.

2. A large class of utterances purport to make reference to phenomena that exist outside of, and independently of, the speaker, the hearer, and their representations, and indeed, in some cases, independently of all representations.

3. Features 1 and 2 require that we understand the utterances of many of these sentences as having truth conditions that are independent of our representations. By purporting to make reference to *public phenomena,* phenomena that are ontologically and not merely epistemically objective, we presuppose that the truth or falsity of the statements is fixed by how the world is, independently of how we represent it.

4. But that presupposition amounts to the claim that there is a way things are that is independent of our representations, and that claim is just (one version of) external realism.

One last way—and perhaps the simplest way—to see this point is to use Brute Force: Put an explicit statement of the denial of the

Background conditions into the speech act itself and see what happens. See, for example, how it contrasts with the denial of standard truth conditions.

If I say:

Mt. Everest has snow and ice near the summit and there is no snow on Mt. Everest.

what I have said is self-contradictory, because the first clause entails the negation of the second. But if I say:

Mt. Everest has snow and ice near the summit, and external reality has never existed.

what I say is literally puzzling. We do not know how to understand it in the normal way, because the second clause doesn't just contradict the first clause but denies a condition that is taken for granted in the normal understanding of the first.

Berkeley and other idealists recognized something very much like this point. Berkeley saw that it was a problem for his account that if each person refers only to his or her own ideas when speaking, then there is a question about how one succeeds in communicating with others. Berkeley's answer was that God guarantees successful communication. This, I believe both Berkeley and I would agree, is not a case of normal understanding in my sense. When I say "snow is white" or "my dog has fleas," I am not normally taken to be relying on God, since even an atheist can attempt to communicate in a public language. Berkeley saw that the price for abandoning external realism was an abandonment of normal understanding, and he was willing to pay the price. One objection to some of the current challenges to realism is that they want to abandon external realism without paying the price. The price of the abandonment of realism is the abandonment of normal understanding. If someone wishes to abandon normal understanding, he or she owes us an account of what sort of understanding is possible.

The Distinction Between Brute Reality and
Socially Constructed Reality

My argument is not yet complete. The argument so far, if valid, is
an answer to phenomenalist idealism but not to social constructionism. What it shows so far is that for a large class of utterances,
each individual utterance requires for its intelligibility a publicly
accessible reality. I have further characterized that reality as representation independent. But there is still an ambiguity. Talk of
money and marriages is talk of a publicly accessible reality, and
such phenomena are "representation independent" in the sense
that this twenty dollar bill or this marriage between Sam and Sally
exists independently of your or my representations of it. After all,
statements about money meet the conditions that there are facts
independent of the speech act that makes them satisfied or unsat-
isfied, e.g., "You owe me five dollars" presupposes an independently existing reality as much as does "Mt. Everest has snow and
ice near the summit." But marriages and money, unlike mountains and atoms, do not exist independently of *all* representations,
and this distinction needs to be made explicit in the account. The
argument so far might be interpreted to allow that all of reality is
socially constructed in the way that, for example, money is socially
constructed. Facts about money can be epistemically objective
even if the existence of money is socially constructed, and, therefore, to that extent, ontologically subjective.

To complete the argument we need to show that within the
class of speech acts that refer to a reality beyond themselves there
is a subclass whose normal understanding requires a reality independent of *all* representation. The simplest way to show that is to
show that a socially constructed reality presupposes a reality independent of all social constructions, because there has to be
something for the construction to be constructed out of. To construct money, property, and language, for example, there have to
be the raw materials of bits of metal, paper, land, sounds, and
marks, for example. And the raw materials cannot in turn be so-

cially constructed without presupposing some even rawer materials out of which they are constructed, until eventually we reach a bedrock of brute physical phenomena independent of all representations. The ontological subjectivity of the socially constructed reality requires an ontologically objective reality out of which it is constructed. To the "transcendental argument" of the previous section—a public language presupposes a public world—we add a "transcendental argument" in this section—a socially constructed reality presupposes a nonsocially constructed reality.

By this stage in the argument I hope the point is obvious. In a sense, one of the main aims of this book has been to spell it out. Because the logical form of the creation of socially constructed reality consists in iterations of the structure X counts as Y in C, the iterations must bottom out in an X element that is not itself an institutional construction. Otherwise you would get infinite regress or circularity. It is a logical consequence of the main argument of the book that you cannot have institutional facts without brute facts.

To conclude the discussion of realism I would like also to show that there is a contrast between the conditions on our normal understanding of statements about brute physical facts and those about institutional facts. To show that there is a class of speech acts that presuppose for their intelligibility a reality beyond *all* representations, let us once again use "Brute Force" and observe the consequences of putting the counterfactual supposition of the denial of the condition into the representation itself. Consider, e.g., the claims

1. Mt. Everest has snow and ice near its summit,

and its negation,

2. It is not the case that Mt. Everest has snow and ice near its summit.

Speech acts of the sort exemplified by claims 1 and 2, so I will argue, purport to state facts that are "ontologically objective" and therefore "representation-independent" in the sense that I have tried to explain. In this respect they differ from, e.g., the claim

3. You owe me five dollars,

and its negation,

4. It is not the case that you owe me five dollars.

We can see the difference if we put the counterfactual supposition into the claims, as follows:

A. In a world that is like ours, except that representations have never existed in it, Mt. Everest has snow and ice near the summit,

and

B. In a world that is like ours, except that representations have never existed in it, it is not the case that Mt. Everest has snow and ice near the summit.

Notice that in A and B, on our normal, naive, intuitive understanding, the supposition of the antecedent does not affect our understanding of the whole statement, as is shown by the fact that the negation of the consequent leaves the status of this type of statement unaffected. The truth or falsity of both A and B depends entirely on the presence or absence of snow and ice near the summit of Mt. Everest, and the presence of snow and ice near the summit of Mt. Everest is in no way dependent on the existence of human or other sorts of representations.

But contrast these cases with

C. In a world that is like ours, except that representations have never existed in it, you owe me five dollars,

and

D. In a world that is like ours, except that representations have never existed in it, it is not the case that you owe me five dollars.

There is a crucial difference between A and B, on the one hand, and C and D, on the other. On our normal understanding, A and B are unaffected by the counterfactual supposition; our understanding is the same and their truth depends entirely on the existence of snow and ice at the summit of Mt Everest. But C, as it stands, is puzzling and even self-defeating in the same way that "There is snow on Mt. Everest and the external world has never existed" is self-defeating, for a condition of the possibility of your owing me money is the existence of certain human rules, practices, and institutions. And this is shown by the fact that if we negate the consequent in C so that we get D, if we could understand the result at all we would have to understand it as a trivial truth: There is no way that anyone could owe anyone anything in a world without representations. To say that you owe me money in a world in which no one ever said or thought anything would be like saying you got a base hit to left center field in the third game of the World Series in a world in which baseball never existed.

To summarize, the claim that I am making is this: Any statement is a representation and therefore to be understood as a statement must be understood as a representation. Statements 1, 2, 3, and 4 all share this feature. But there is a difference between statements 1 and 2, on the one hand, and 3 and 4 on the other. 1 and 2 purport to represent mind-independent features of the world and therefore do not require the existence of representations in the world as part of the conditions of their normal intelligibility. Statements 3 and 4, on the other hand, purport to be about representation-dependent features of the world and therefore do require the existence of representations as part of the conditions of their normal intelligibility. You can see this by considering the normal understanding of sentences where 1, 2, 3, and 4 are embedded in sentences expressing a counterfactual supposition of the nonexistence of any representations, A, B, C, and D. On our normal understanding, the truth value of 1 and 2 is unaffected; the truth value of 3 and 4 is affected decisively. On the supposition, 3 becomes self-defeating, almost self-contradictory; 4, if intelligible at all, becomes trivially true. Thus, on our normal understanding, statements about money require the existence of representations as part of their conditions of normal intelligibility. Statements about mountains are entirely free of any such requirement.

The upshot then is that there is a contrast between the role of the presupposition of external realism and the presupposition of the existence of human representations in normal understanding. Normal understanding of talk of both money and mountains requires external realism, but normal understanding of talk of money presupposes the existence of representations in a way that normal understanding of mountains does not. Money is understood as socially constructed; mountains are not understood as socially constructed.

Strengths and Limitations of the Foregoing Arguments

This aim of this chapter has been to show that our ordinary linguistic practices presuppose external realism, just as the aim of Chapter 7 was to show that certain arguments against that presupposition do not work. Now I want to say what is and what is not proved by the "transcendental arguments" in this part.

1. I have not demonstrated that external realism is true. I have tried to show that it is presupposed by the use of very large sections of a public language. If you take yourself to be communicating with others in the normal way in the sort of speech acts I have given as examples, you are committed to external realism. I have not shown that there is a real world but only that you are committed to its existence when you talk to me or to anyone else.

2. An alternative is always solipsism, the view that my mental states are the only things that exist. I have not refuted solipsism; that is, I have not refuted solipsism for me. Only remember: Your

solipsism is instantly refuted by me; mine—assuming that you exist—instantly refuted by you.

3. I have not shown that we all have a belief or are committed to a belief in realism. On the contrary, realism is part of the Background; and when functioning the Background is not a matter of any intentional states at all. One of the keys to understanding the Background is this: One can be committed to the truth of a proposition without having any beliefs, thoughts, assumptions, hypotheses, or other "propositional attitudes" regarding that proposition at all. "Taking something for granted" need not name a psychological state. Pretheoretically we take external realism for granted, and for that reason it need not be a belief, but is prior to having beliefs.

4. There is nothing epistemic about the arguments. I am not saying that in order to *know the truth* of our claims we have to presuppose realism. My argument is completely independent of questions of knowledge or even of truth. On my account, falsehood stands as much in need of the real world as does truth. The claim, to repeat, is about conditions of *intelligibility,* not about conditions of *knowledge.*[14]

5. The arguments only apply to utterances for which there is a normal understanding. Famously, there is no normal understanding of quantum mechanics or the set theoretical paradoxes. The struggles over the interpretation of quantum mechanics are, at least in part, an attempt to provide a normal understanding of these claims. Not every proposition about the world has a normal understanding.

6. There is nothing self-guaranteeing about normal understanding. Sometimes we are forced to revise our normal understanding because of new discoveries. This happened in the case of color statements. Pretheoretically we think of colors as intrinsic

features of objects; but physics tells us that as far as color is concerned, the only intrinsic feature of an object is that it differentially scatters and absorbs the various wavelengths of light. These light/matter interactions are detected by our nervous system, producing the experiences that we interpret as color. In such a case, we replace one normal understanding with another. But notice that the replacement (and presumably correct) normal understanding presupposes ER as much as did the earlier (presumably mistaken) normal understanding. To put this point very crudely: the discovery that colors as such are not a part of the external world does not threaten our presupposition of the existence of the external world, because we still rely on the external world to give our backup account of the subjective illusion of color. Similar remarks could be made about, for example, solidity. The prospects of refuting ER by appealing to the history of science would appear to be doomed to failure, because the history is one of replacing a mistaken normal understanding, where an apparently ontologically objective phenomenon is shown to be really subjective, with an account given in terms of phenomena that supposedly really are objective.

7. If my argument is correct, it should go part of the way toward explaining our embarrassment in the face of demands to prove the existence of the real world, and the inadequacy of existing proofs. I think it does this. Once we start talking to our interlocutors we have already presupposed the existence of the real world, and we are embarrassed to try to prove what our attempts at proof already presuppose.

I conclude this chapter by answering the following question: Why does it matter? What difference does it make? After all, as Wittgenstein says somewhere, it is possible to construe these great debates between realism and antirealism, between idealism and materialism as just so many battle cries. The antirealist nonetheless takes his car to a mechanic to get it fixed and brushes his teeth, just as if he believed they were objects in the external world.

So what difference does it make whether or not one says that one is a realist or an antirealist?

I actually think that philosophical theories make a tremendous difference to every aspect of our lives. In my observation, the rejection of realism, the denial of ontological objectivity, is an essential component of the attacks on epistemic objectivity, rationality, truth, and intelligence in contemporary intellectual life. It is no accident that the various theories of language, literature, and even education that try to undermine the traditional conceptions of truth, epistemic objectivity, and rationality rely heavily on arguments against external realism. The first step in combating irrationalism—not the only step but the first step—is a refutation of the arguments against external realism and a defense of external realism as a presupposition of large areas of discourse.

9
Truth and Correspondence

My investigation into the nature of social reality has proceeded by investigating the status of the facts in virtue of which our statements about social reality are true. As a final matter of philosophical housekeeping, in order to justify that procedure I will in this chapter defend the idea that truth is a matter of correspondence to facts. In earlier chapters I asked questions about the nature and structure of such facts as the fact that this is a five dollar bill or that I am a citizen of the United States. If skeptical arguments against the existence of facts or against the correspondence between true statements and facts were really valid, then this aspect of my enterprise would at the very least need to be recast. My conception of social reality does not logically require the correspondence theory of truth—someone could reject the correspondence theory and still accept my analysis—but the overall picture I, in fact, hold proceeds by way of external realism through the correspondence theory to the structure of social reality, and I am now expounding that picture.

I realize that a full-scale analysis of truth, facts, and correspondence deserves more space than I will give here, but I have a more limited aim than providing a general analysis. My aim is to justify (a version of) the correspondence theory as a methodological tool for the investigation of social facts. However, to do even that, I am going to have to offer what could, with certain qualifications, be called a theory of truth, and this requires that I answer some rival theories.

This chapter has three parts. First, I present the intuitive idea of truth as correspondence to the facts. Second, I review a set of objections to this theory, made by Strawson and others. Third, I offer a general account of the relations of truth, fact, correspondence, and disquotation that I then use to answer the Strawson style of objections. Finally, in an appendix to the chapter I answer the "slingshot argument" against the correspondence theory.

The Intuitive Idea of Truth as Correspondence

In general, statements are attempts to describe how things are in the world, which exists independently of the statement.[1] The statement will be true or false depending on whether things in the world really are the way the statement says they are. Truth, in short, is a matter of accuracy of a certain sort of linguistic representation. So, for example, the statement that hydrogen atoms have one electron, or that the earth is ninety-three million miles from the sun, or that my dog is now in the kitchen are true or false depending on whether or not things in the hydrogen atom, solar system, and domestic canine line of business, respectively, really are the way these statements say they are. Truth, so construed, admits of degrees. That statement about the sun, for example, is only *roughly true*.

In some versions this idea is called the correspondence theory of truth. It is often presented as an account of "true" thus:

A statement is true if and only if it corresponds to the facts.

But if this is supposed to be an explanation of "true," we need to be told a bit more about what is meant by "correspond" and "fact." I believe the best way to begin to understand these notions is to start with an idea that is often supposed to count *against* the correspondence theory. Here is the idea: It is often said that any account of truth has to meet the condition that,

For any sentence s,

s is true if and only if p

where for "s" we put some specification of a sentence, e.g., by quotation, "Snow is white," and for "p" we put the sentence itself. We thus get, as a substitution instance of the formula,

"Snow is white" is true if and only if snow is white.

This criterion of truth is sometimes called "disquotation,"[2] because the sentence quoted on the left-hand side occurs on the right with the quotation marks dropped. The substitution instances have come to be called "T sentences." The disquotation criterion requires some modification to deal with indexical sentences such as "I am hungry," and purists will want to make careful distinctions among sentences, statements, and propositions—distinctions that are not apparent in the disquotational criterion as stated above. Furthermore, we need to modify disquotation to allow for truth ascribed in a metalanguage to sentences in an object language that is not included in the metalanguage. For example,

"Schnee ist weiß" is true in German iff snow is white.

But it is possible to make the modifications to deal with all these problems. About an indexical sentence such as "I am hungry," for example, we can say

"I am hungry" said by a speaker S at a time t is true iff S is hungry at t.

About cases where the metalanguage does not include the object language, we can say that the sentence on the right-hand side must be a translation of or express the same proposition as the sentence quoted on the left. And the distinctions among sentences, statements, and propositions can be preserved within the framework of the disquotational criterion, so for the sake of this argument I will ignore indexicals and ignore the distinctions except where they are essential to the argument.

In our example, the quoted sentence on the left-hand side, "Snow is white," specifies a sentence by exhibiting it; and the right-hand side specifies the condition that must be satisfied if the sentence is true; it specifies that *in virtue of which* the sentence is true, or—what amounts to the same thing—that which *makes the sentence true,* if it is true, and it does this by simply repeating the very same sentence. This makes disquotation look trivial. But for our present purposes there are at least two important ideas in the disquotational criterion. First, sentences are made true in virtue of satisfying a condition that stands outside the sentence. And second, for a large number of cases we can specify the condition that makes the sentence true just by repeating the sentence.

We need a noun or noun phrase to name all those conditions that make sentences true, all those truth makers specified on the right-hand side of T sentences, in virtue of which sentences are true, if they are true. The word "fact"—as well as in some uses "situation" and "state of affairs"—has evolved as the general term that names the truth makers, and "corresponds" is just a general term to name all the various ways in which sentences are made true in virtue of facts. *On a natural interpretation, the disquotational criterion of truth, together with the appropriate understanding of the notions of "fact" and "correspondence," imply the correspondence theory of truth, because if the quoted sentence on the left-hand side of a T sentence really is true, then it must correspond to the fact stated on the right-hand side.* Part of my aim in this chapter is to explain that "appropriate understanding."

If, as I have said, the correspondence theory is implicit in the disquotational criterion, we ought to be able to spell out the implication. I will argue in more detail later for the various steps, but in a preliminary formulation, here they are.

1. Assume disquotation:

> For any s, s is true iff p.

2. Given the appropriate replacements for "s" and "p" in the above formula, the right-hand side of a T sentence specifies a condition that is satisfied if and only if the sentence specified on the left-hand side is true.

3. We need a general name for those conditions when satisfied, and that name, among others, is "fact."

4. We need a verb to name the variety of ways in which sentences, when true, relate to facts in a way that makes them true; and that verb, among others, is "correspond."

5. With these understandings, from the disquotational criterion we get a version of the correspondence theory:

> For any s, s is true iff s corresponds to the fact that p.

I should make it clear immediately that the correspondence theory is not an attempt to define "true" without using other semantic notions. If we tried to take this account as a *definition* of "true" in nonsemantic terms, it would be circular because it uses such semantically loaded notions as "fact" and "correspond."

I hope everything I have said so far sounds obvious, because I think it really is obvious. However, I have to tell you that these points are routinely denied, and many philosophers think disquotation somehow militates against the correspondence theory. There are deep philosophical issues in all of this, because for reasons I will explain later, we have deep philosophical urges to misunderstand all these points. I will return to these issues below.

Strawson's Objections to the Correspondence Theory

Over forty years ago there was a famous debate between Austin and Strawson about truth and facts.[3] It was generally accepted that Strawson won the argument. Many of Strawson's objections were to specific details of Austin's version of the correspondence theory, but he also presented general objections applicable to other versions of the theory; and he concluded that "The correspondence theory requires not purification but elimination."[4] His claim is not that it is false to say that a true statement is one that corresponds to the facts, but rather that the correspondence theory gives us a false picture of the use of the word "true" and of the nature of facts. The picture it gives us is that facts are kinds of complex things or events or groups of things, and that "truth" names a special relation of correspondence between statements and these nonlinguistic entities. He says, "It is the misrepresentation of 'correspondence between statement and fact' *as a relation, of any kind, between events or things or groups of things* that is the trouble."[5]

I agree with many features of Strawson's account. In fact for many years I was convinced that it presented decisive objections to the correspondence theory. In what follows I will try both to summarize it and to strengthen it with some added considerations in the same spirit. Nonetheless, I will argue in the next section that Strawson's argument, even as strengthened, does not show the need to eliminate the correspondence theory.

There is a certain picture naturally suggested by the correspondence theory, and that picture, Strawson argues, is false. The picture is that when we ascertain the truth of a statement, we have, on the one hand, the statement, e.g. "The cat is on the mat," and on the other hand, we have the complex thing or group of things, the fact that the cat is on the mat. To ascertain truth we then compare statement and fact to see whether they really do correspond. On this conception facts are kinds of complex objects or events, and correspondence is a matching or picturing relation between the elements of the statement and the elements of the fact.

Historically, it is no accident that the correspondence theory of truth has gone hand in hand with the picture theory of meaning, the theory that sentences have the meanings they do because they are conventionalized pictures of facts. The classic statement of this conception is in Wittgenstein's *Tractatus*.[6] This conception of the correspondence theory has notorious problems. For example, even if it is plausible to think of the fact that the cat is on the mat as a complex of cat and mat and their relation, what about the fact that the cat is not on the mat? Or the fact that there are no three-headed cats? Or the fact that if the cat had been on the mat the dog would have had to have been in the kitchen? Russell in a letter to the young Wittgenstein: "Are there negative facts?" Wittgenstein back: "Of course not!"

This picture engendered by the correspondence theory, the picture that facts are complex objects or events and that truth consists of a kind of matching or isomorphism between the elements of the statement and the elements of the fact is absurd. Once we have identified the statement and the fact, we have nothing further to do by way of comparing them, because the only way to identify a fact is to make a true statement. Once we have answered the question "Which fact?" we have already established truth, because, according to Strawson, there are not two independent entities, the true statement and the fact. Rather, "facts are what statements (when true) state; they are not what statements are about."[7] Facts are not things in the world independent of language; rather, the word "fact," like the words "statement" and "true" themselves, has a certain type of word-world–relating discourse built into it. Facts in short are not extralinguistic things, but facts already have the notions of statement and truth built into them, because in order to specify a fact we have to state a true statement.[8]

Frege thought that facts just *are* true propositions.[9] And the internal logical connection between true statements or true propositions and facts certainly makes that view appealing. After all, the internal logical connection between winnings and victories shows that there are not two separate types of events, winnings and victories. Rather, whenever one wins, one wins a victory because victories just are winnings. Analogously could we say, The internal logical connection between true statements and facts shows that there are *not* two types of phenomena, true statements and facts; but rather, whenever one states truly, one states a fact, because facts just are true statements? But this is a mistake and Strawson avoids making it. He says, "It would be wrong—but not for Mr. Austin's reasons—to identify 'fact' and 'true statement'; for these expressions have different roles in our language."[10] Strawson does not develop the argument, but in any case it could not be right to say that facts just are true statements, because, for example, facts function causally in a way that true statements do not. For example, "The fact that Napoleon failed to perceive the danger to his left flank caused his defeat"[11] makes good sense, whereas "The true statement that Napoleon failed to perceive the danger to his left flank caused his defeat" either makes no sense at all or means something totally different.

But Strawson does insist that there is an internal relation between facts and true statements, and that relation is such that there could not be a genuine relation of correspondence between two independent entities. Our model of a genuine relational statement would be something like

Seattle is north of Portland.

To find out whether such a relation obtains we might first identify Seattle, then identify Portland, and then see whether they really stand in the relation of the former being north of the latter. But we can't do that with the alleged relation of correspondence between statements and facts, because in order to identify the fact we already have to state the corresponding true statement. The "relation" of fact to true statement is internal in a way that is typical of entities referred to by nouns that are internal accusatives of their corresponding verbs.

> The statement that the cat is on the mat corresponds to the
> fact that the cat is on the mat

should be understood not on the genuine relational model exemplified by

> Seattle is north of Portland,

but on the model of such pseudorelational internal accusative sentences as

> Sam won a victory

or

> Sally struck a blow.

Grammatically, "fact" is the internal accusative for "state truly," just as "victory" is the internal accusative for "win" and "blow" the internal accusative for "strike." In none of these cases are there genuine relations between the entity named by the subject of the sentence and the pseudoentity referred to by the direct object.

Furthermore, if the correspondence theory were correct, then it would seem to follow that after we have located the fact that the cat is on the mat and the statement that the cat is on the mat, to establish that the statement is true we would still have to compare the statement with the fact to see that the statement really did correspond to the fact. But the idea is absurd. Once we have identified a fact, we have already identified a true statement. To summarize, Strawson concludes not that the statement "True statements correspond to facts" is false but that the philosophical theory engendered by this tautology is false. Specifically, this philosophical theory makes the false claims that facts are nonlinguistic entities and truth names a relation of correspondence between the linguistic and the nonlinguistic.

In the next section I will argue that Strawson is right to point out the internal connection between fact and true statement but that this does not show that facts are in any sense linguistic entities, or that there is no relation of correspondence between true statements and facts.

Truth, Facts, Disquotation, and Correspondence

I want to begin by noting an odd feature of the current literature: very little of it is concerned with the fact that "true" and "false" are evaluative terms used to describe certain kinds of success and failure. They are used to assess success or failure of statements (and beliefs) in achieving what I call the word-(or mind)-to-world direction of fit. If you read much of the literature, in spite of its technical sophistication, you are left with the question, "So what?" "Why should we care about truth, if that is all it amounts to?" The standard accounts do not explain why truth matters so much to us. I want to offer an account that will, at least in part, explain why it does.

In the first section, I briefly sketched the correspondence theory of truth by showing how it could be construed as a natural consequence of the disquotation criterion for truth. On the correspondence theory, a statement p is true if and only if the statement p corresponds to a fact. On the disquotational theory, for any sentence s used to make a statement p, s is true if and only if p. I suggested that these two criteria of truth are at bottom the same, because if the sentence quoted on the left-hand side of the T sentence is true, then it is true because it corresponds to the fact stated on the right-hand side.

But not all philosophers agree with me about that. To many, these two criteria for truth do not always appear to give the same result. Disquotation makes it look as if the word "true" doesn't really add anything to the original statement. It appears that saying "It's true that the cat is on the mat" is just another way of say-

ing "The cat is on the mat," so it seems that the word "true" is redundant. For this reason the disquotation criterion has inspired
the "redundancy theory of truth," the theory that the word "true"
is redundant, describing nothing. Several philosophers who are
impressed by the redundancy argument have pointed out that
"true" is not *quite* redundant, because we still need it as a shorthand for stating infinite sets of disquotations, for saying such
things as, e.g., "From true premises only true conclusions can be
validly derived." But they nonetheless adhere to a "deflationary" or
"minimalist" theory of truth, the theory that says there is really no
property or relation denoted by "true." The entire content of the
notion of truth is given by disquotation.[12] The first criterion, the
correspondence criterion, makes it look as if there is a genuine
relation between two independently identified entities—the statement and the fact, and "true" describes this relation. Disquotation
appears to imply the redundancy theory, or at least the deflationary theory, and redundancy theories and deflationary theories are
standardly supposed to be inconsistent with the correspondence
theory. And we have seen in our discussion of Strawson's views
that there are very serious objections to the correspondence theory.

So the defender of the correspondence theory is left with two
sets of questions: First, can we make a substantive conception of
the correspondence theory consistent with the disquotation criterion? By "a substantive conception" I mean a conception according to which there really are nonlinguistic facts in the world and
statements are true because they really do stand in certain relations to these facts, relations that we variously describe as fitting,
matching, stating, or corresponding to the facts. And second, can
we answer Strawson's objections to the correspondence theory?

To answer these questions I will make some general observations about the ordinary use of the expressions "true" and "fact"
and about how they might have evolved their present meaning.
My investigation at this point is a Wittgensteinian-style enterprise
into the language games we play with these words, and its aim is

to remove the false pictures that our misunderstandings of the language games engender. The next few paragraphs are intended as observations about word usage with some etymological speculations about how those usages might have evolved.

"True" comes from the same etymological root as "trust" and "trustworthy," and all these from the Indo-European root "*deru*" for "tree," suggesting uprightness and reliability generally. There are not only true statements but true friends (real or genuine friends), true emotions (sincerely felt, not fake), true heirs (rightful or legitimate), as well as true north, true trout (the eastern brook trout is not a true trout; it is a char), knives that cut true, and true believers.

These various senses of "true" show family resemblances. If truth has some general connection to trustworthiness and reliability, we need to ask: Under what conditions would we find a statement trustworthy or reliable? Obviously when it does what it purports to do, that is, when it accurately states how things are. When it says things are thus and so, then it is reliable if and only if things really are thus and so. This is how we get the disquotation criterion for truth. The disquotation criterion gives us a general criterion of truth that is consistent with our intuition that truth implies accuracy, reliability, and trustworthiness. Aristotle articulated this conception when he said that to speak the truth is to say of what is that it is, and to say of what is not that it is not. In short, "truth" applied to statements is a term of assessment implying trustworthiness, and disquotation gives us a criterion of trustworthiness.

Now let us turn to "fact." We know definitely that this word is derived from Latin "*factum*," which is the neuter past particle of the verb "*facere*," meaning "to do" or "to make." Hence, to mix three languages, one can say that the *factum* is the *thing done,* or the *fait accompli.* But so far this has no obvious connection with true statements. Here is the connection. Just as we need a general term, "true," for the feature of trustworthiness as it applies to statements, so we need a general term for what makes statements trustworthy, for what it is in virtue of which they are reliable. If it is true that the cat is on the mat, there must be something in virtue of which it is true, something that makes it true. The disquotation criterion only tells us *for each case* what that something is. The something that makes it true that the cat is on the mat is just that the cat is on the mat. And so on for any true statement. What makes it true that grass is green is that grass is green, etc. *But we still need a general term for all those somethings, for what makes it true that grass is green, that snow is white, that 2 + 2 = 4 and all the rest. "Fact" has evolved to fill this need.* The word "fact" in English has come to mean (fairly recently, by the way) that in virtue of which true statements are true. This is why Strawson is right to think that in order to specify a fact, in order to answer the question "which fact?" we have to state a true statement. When it comes to specifying their essence, facts can only be stated and not named.

But it does not follow that facts are somehow essentially linguistic, that they have the notion of statement somehow built into them. On the contrary, on the account I have given they are precisely not linguistic (except, of course, for the small but important class of linguistic facts) because the whole point of having the notion of "fact" is to have a notion for that which stands outside the statement but which makes it true, or in virtue of which it is true, if it is true. On this account facts are not complex objects, nor are they linguistic entities; rather, they are *conditions*, specifically, they are conditions in the world that satisfy the truth conditions expressed by statements. The word "condition" has the usual process-product ambiguity; in this case the ambiguity is between the *requirement* and the *thing required*. The statement determines a truth condition as requirement, and if satisfied there will be something in the world as the thing required.[13] For example, the statement that the cat is on the mat expresses the truth condition as requirement. If the statement is true, there will be a condition in the world that meets the requirement, and that condition is the fact that the cat is on the mat. On this account we do not

have or need a thick metaphysical notion of "fact." Anything sufficient to make a statement true is a fact. Thus the fact that there are
no three-headed cats is as much a fact as the fact that the cat is
on the mat. Consider the miniworld described in Chapter 7, consisting of a number of circular objects. Is it a fact in that world
that there are no cats? Of course. This is just another way of saying that the miniworld satisfies the condition that there are no
cats in it.

For this reason, because of the definitional connection between
fact and true statement, there could not be an inconsistency between the correspondence criterion of truth and the disquotational criterion. "Fact" is just defined as that in virtue of which a
statement is true, and disquotation gives *the form* of what makes
each statement true by simply repeating the statement. But if the
statement is true, then repeating it is just the same as stating
the fact. The disquotational criterion tells us that the statement
"The cat is on the mat" is true if and only if the cat is on the mat. The
correspondence criterion tells us that the statement "The cat is on
the mat" is true if and only if it corresponds to a fact. But which
fact? The only fact it could correspond to, if true, is the fact that
the cat is on the mat. But that is precisely the result given by the
disquotational criterion, because that is the fact stated by the
right-hand side of the T sentence: the statement "The cat is on
the mat" is true if and only if the cat is on the mat. And this is also
why in order to know that it is true that the cat is on the mat, all we
have to do is establish that the cat is on the mat. We don't have to
establish *in addition* that the statement that the cat is on the mat
corresponds to the fact that the cat is on the mat, because we have
already established that correspondence when we established
that the cat is on the mat.

With these points about "true" and "fact" in mind, let us turn
our attention to "correspondence." In what sense if any do true
statements *correspond* to facts? Even if we grant that facts, though
they have to be propositionally specified, are still not linguistic entities, all the same is there any sense to the notion of correspon-

dence? How do we answer Strawson's objections on that score?

We need a general word for assessing success and failure in achieving fit for representations that have the word-to-world direction of fit, and those words, among others less important, are "true" and "false." We also need a general term for naming all those somethings specified on the right-hand side of T sentences when the sentence specified on the left-hand side is true; that word is "fact." But grammatically we now need a verb for describing the relations between the statements and the facts when the statements are true.

Statements are true if and only if they blank the facts.

We need a word for "blank," and it should be just empty enough and vague enough to allow for all the different kind of ways in which statements can blank the facts, in ways that render the statement true. In English there are a number of such verbs: "fit," "match," "describe," and "correspond to" are four. Just as we need a general term for all the different features of the world that can make statements true, so we need a general term for naming the ways in which true statements can accurately represent how things are in the world, and "corresponds to the facts" is just such a general characterization. "Corresponds to the facts" is just a shorthand for the variety of ways in which statements can accurately represent how things are, and that variety is the same as the variety of statements, or more strictly speaking, the variety of assertive speech acts. Furthermore, we need to allow for the fact that statements can be *approximately* true or *roughly* true. For example, the statement that the earth is ninety-three million miles from the sun is only approximately true. In such a case the statement only *approximately* fits or corresponds to the facts.

So both the correspondence theory and the disquotational theory are true, and they are not in conflict. The correspondence theory is trivially true, but it misleads us because we think facts must be some complex kinds of material objects, and "correspondence" must name some very general relation of resemblance, or at least isomorphism, between statements and the complex entities that are facts.

I believe that Strawson was right to think that the correspondence theory engenders a false picture. However, that false picture is not a logical consequence of the correspondence theory properly understood; the picture is rather a classic example of how we are misled by the surface grammar of words and sentences when we fail to look at the actual use of the expressions involved. It is a classic example of being confused by not understanding the use of words, and it invites Wittgensteinian-style philosophical therapy. We think that since "fact" is a noun and since nouns name objects, then facts must be complicated kinds of objects; we think that correspondence must imply some kind of isomorphism, and then we are puzzled about negative facts, hypothetical facts, etc. But once we understand the logic of the words involved, we see that facts are not complicated objects, and that there is no necessary isomorphism between the syntactical structure of true statements and the structure of facts. Furthermore, we see that there is no problem about negatives, hypotheticals, etc. The true statement that the cat is not on the mat corresponds to the fact that the cat is not on the mat. What else? And what goes for negative statements goes for all the rest. If it is true that if the cat had been on the mat, then the dog would have had to have been in the kitchen, then it must be a fact that if the cat had been on the mat, then the dog would have had to have been in the kitchen. For every true statement there is a corresponding fact, because that is how these words are defined.

The hardest thing to keep in mind in this whole discussion is that we are dealing with a small bunch of tautologies and their entailments. Disquotation and the correspondence theory are trivially, tautologically true; hence, any appearance of conflict must derive from our urge to misunderstand them. Just as the correspondence theory generates a false picture because we do not adequately understand the actual use of these words, so disquotation generates a false picture, and for the same reason. The false picture generated by disquotation is that there is no property of truth at all: "Snow is white" is true iff snow is white. "Grass is green" is true iff grass is green, and so on for every indicative sentence. On this view, there is no common property of truth, nothing in common to all these cases; there is nothing in common to both "Snow is white" and "Grass is green" in virtue of which they are both true.

I want to call attention to what a wildly counterintuitive result this is. Most philosophers would not think of saying about other sorts of formal terms such as number words, e.g., "two," or formal evaluative terms, e.g., "good," that nothing whatever can be said about what they mean other than that certain purely syntactical constraints are imposed on their application. But many philosophers are content to adopt redundancy or deflationary conceptions of truth. They claim there is nothing whatever in common to all true statements except that they satisfy the disquotation criterion. There is no *content* to the notion of truth, except the bare minimum content that uses of "true" must satisfy disquotation; they must satisfy the condition that s is true iff p, where for "s" we substitute the specification of a sentence and for "p" we substitute *that very sentence or some translation of it.*

Why would anyone adopt such a counterintuitive view? The illusion of redundancy derives entirely from the fact that on the disquotation criterion the left-hand side looks like the right-hand side except for the occurrence of the quotation marks and the word "true." So it seems that saying "'Snow is white' is true" is just a long-winded way of saying "Snow is white." The one is just a syntactical variant of the other with no change in semantic content. But that conclusion does not follow. We need words to describe success and failure in achieving fit for statements, just as we need words for describing success and failure in achieving fit for orders. The words for statements are "true" and "false"; the words for orders are "obeyed" and "disobeyed." The statement has to determine its own truth conditions, just as the order has to determine its own obedience conditions. But to state the truth conditions of the statement we need just repeat the statement, whereas to state the obedience conditions of the order we do not restate the order. This asymmetry derives from the fact that the *statement* of truth conditions is a statement, but the statement of obedience condition for an order is not an order; it too is a statement. So the illusion of redundancy is engendered by the fact that stating truth conditions for statements is different from stating conditions of satisfaction for other sorts of speech acts. I explore this idea further in the next section.

Designing a Language

Another way to make these same points is with the following thought experiment: Suppose you were designing a language for beings that did not already have one. What would you put in? I mean after you have a syntax for constructing sentences, expressions for the quantifiers and logical connectives, and words for "dog" and "cat," "red" and "blue," etc., what general structural features would you put in? Well, for starters you would need to put in devices for performing the various standard kinds of speech acts, such as statements, questions, commands, and promises. To do this you would need ways of marking the distinction between the propositional content and the illocutionary force of the speech act; that is, you need to be able to distinguish among "Leave the room!," an order, "Will you leave the room?," a question, and "You will leave the room," a prediction. These are three different speech acts with three different illocutionary forces, but all contain the same propositional content: that you will leave the room.

Because the different illocutionary forces relate the propositional content to the real world in different ways, with different directions of fit, you need different words to mark success or failure in achieving the fit between the proposition and the real world. Thus you would need a word to mark the fact that orders are *obeyed* or *disobeyed*. Orders are obeyed when the person ordered does the thing she is ordered to do because she was ordered to do it. Orders have the world-to-word direction of fit, because part of the point of the order is to try to make the world change to match the words. Similarly, promises are *kept* or *fulfilled* when the promisor does what he promises to do because he promised to do it. Promises also have the world-to-word direction of fit, because part of the point of the promise is to try to make the world change to match the words.

Just as orders and promises achieve or fail to achieve fit between the propositional content and reality, so do statements. But statements have a different direction of fit because the aim of the statement is to get its propositional content to match an independently existing reality, not to change reality to match the propositional content. To the extent that statements succeed or fail in the match, we say that they are *true* or *false*, and any language we might design will need words to mark these forms of success and failure. It will need words for truth and falsity.

But the criterion of success of the speech act in achieving fit will be stated differently for, on the one hand, statements, which have the word-to-world direction of fit than for, on the other hand, promises and orders, which have the world-to-word direction of fit. The conditions of satisfaction of the statement that you will leave the room are that you will leave the room. The statement of the truth conditions is just a restatement of the statement, and this result, as we have seen, is the disquotational criterion of truth. For any statement, to state the conditions of satisfaction or success in achieving fit, you need only restate the statement. But the statement of the obedience conditions of the order "Leave the room!" cannot be stated disquotationally in the form: leave the room!, because the statement of the conditions of satisfaction of the order has a different direction of fit from the order itself. To state the obedience conditions of an order, you have to make a statement, e.g.,

The order O, "Leave the room!," made by a speaker S to a hearer H at a time t is obeyed iff H leaves the room at t because of O.

Hence it looks as if "true" is somehow redundant in a way that "obeyed" and "kept" are not redundant. But this is an illusion. "True" and "false" are the crucial terms for assessing success in achieving fit in the mode appropriate to statements, just as "obeyed" and "disobeyed" assess success in achieving fit in the manner appropriate to orders.

Moreover, you will need terms to mark what is on the other side of the direction of fit, on the world side. In the case of orders and promises, this is easy. You need words for the various *actions* that constitute obedience to orders, fulfillment of promises, etc. Actions do not need orders and promises to exist, but orders and promises need actions to be obeyed or kept. But on the other side of statements, a word for "action" is not enough and even words for "object" and "event" will not be enough. Why not? Because the disquotation criterion for success in achieving fit requires that the conditions on the world side of the word-to-world fit be specified by using a syntactical form appropriate for expressing whole propositions. In short, you need a word for "fact." You need a word for the nonlinguistic correlate of the statement in virtue of which, or because of which, the statement is true, and that word must take syntactic completions appropriate to match statements; they must have a form like "the fact that . . . ," where what follows the "that" is just the expression of the propositional content of the statement. Facts don't need statements in order to exist, but statements need facts in order to be true.

So now in your invented language you have words for "true," "statements," and "fact." It would be nice to have a general verb to describe the relations between them, a verb that was neutral about all the specific forms of statements and the variety of ways in which true statements relate to facts. About as general and empty a verb for this as you can come up with in English is "correspond," so it would be useful to have a word equivalent to this, and you can then state the definitional relations between these notions by saying something equivalent to

Statements are true if and only if they correspond to the facts.

I believe that this thought experiment, though it leaves out many complexities, describes the situation we are actually in with our use of the words "true," "statement," and "fact."

Summary and Conclusion

I will now draw together the various threads of this discussion. I want to summarize the foregoing in a way that will explain some of the methodological features of the earlier chapters.

1. "True" is the adjective for assessing statements (as well as, e.g., beliefs, that like statements have the mind-to-world or word-to-world direction of fit). Statements are assessed as true when they are trustworthy, i.e., when the way they represent things as being is the way that things really are.

2. The criterion of reliability is given by disquotation. This makes it look as if "true" is redundant, but it is not. We need a metalinguistic predicate for assessing success in achieving the word-to-world direction of fit, and that term is "true."

3. The assignment of "truc" to statements is not arbitrary. In general, statements are true in virtue of conditions in the world that are not parts of the statement. Statements are made true by how things are in the world that is independent of the statement. We need general terms to name these how-things-are-in-the-world, and "fact" is one such term. Others are "situation" and "state of affairs."

4. Because statements determine their own truth conditions and because the term "fact" refers to that in virtue of which statements are true, the canonical way to specify the fact is the same as the way to specify the statement, by stating it. This specification requires a whole clause; hence, both statements and facts are

specified propositionally, "the fact that . . ." and "the statement that . . . ," but facts are not thereby linguistic in nature.

5. Because the identity of the fact is dependent on the specific features of the fact being the same as those specified by the corresponding statement and in virtue of which the corresponding statement is true, it is false to suppose that the context "the fact that p" must preserve identity of reference under substitution of logically equivalent sentences for p. For further discussion of this point, see the Appendix to this chapter.

6. What about the substitution of coreferring expressions? In some cases, substitution of coreferring expressions can preserve identity of fact. Because Tully was identical with Cicero, then intuitively, the fact that Tully was an orator is the very same fact as the fact that Cicero was an orator. Why? Because exactly the same state of affairs in the world makes each statement true, and "fact" is defined as that which makes a statement true.

But in general, substitution of coreferring definite descriptions does not yield reference to the same fact. Intuitively, the fact that Tully was an orator is a different fact from the fact that the man who denounced Catiline was an orator, even though Tully is the man who denounced Catiline. Why? Because the latter fact requires that someone have denounced Catiline for its existence, and the existence of the former fact has no such requirement.

7. Facts are not the same as true statements. There are several ways to demonstrate this. Here are two. First it makes sense to speak of facts functioning causally in a way it does not make sense to speak of true statements functioning causally. Second, the relation of a fact to statements is one-many since the same fact may be stated by different statements. For example, the same fact is stated by "Cicero was an orator" and "Tully was an orator."

8. Wherever there is disquotation there are also alternative ways of describing or specifying the facts. Thus the true statement "Sally is the sister of Sam" corresponds to the fact that Sally is the

sister of Sam, but there are further things to be said, e.g., that Sally is female, and that Sally and Sam have the same father and mother. Many philosophical disputes are about the structure of facts, and in general these issues go far beyond disquotation. For example, the philosophical disputes about color, and other secondary qualities, are about the nature of the facts that correspond to such claims as that this object is red, and the analysis of such facts requires more than disquotation.

9. One (only one) method in philosophy is to analyze the structure of the facts that make our statements true. In earlier chapters I have attempted to do that with the structure of social and institutional facts.

APPENDIX TO CHAPTER 9: THE SLINGSHOT ARGUMENT

There is another argument against the correspondence theory of truth that, if valid, would be disastrous for the theory. It is a technical-sounding argument originally attributed to Frege, used by Quine against modal logic, and recently revived by Donald Davidson against the correspondence theory; it has come to be called "the slingshot argument" (presumably because such a little David of an argument can be used to slay such huge Goliaths as modal logic and the correspondence theory). It is usually stated with breathtaking speed,[14] but if we are going to explore its weaknesses we will need to slow down and go through it in low gear.

The point of the argument is to show that if a true statement corresponds to a fact, it corresponds to any and every fact; hence, the notion of correspondence is completely empty. If statements correspond, then all true statements correspond to the same thing. The argument can be stated in the following steps. (I have put my own comments on the steps in parentheses.)

Step 1. Assumption: The statement that snow is white corresponds to the fact that snow is white.

This statement is a substitution instance of the correspondence theory, and the aim of the argument is to refute the theory by reducing the statement to absurdity.

Step 2. Assumption: In contexts such as Step 1, the occurrence of sentences and singular terms is such that (a) the whole statement preserves truth under the substitution of coreferring singular terms, and (b) it preserves truth under the substitution of logically equivalent sentences.

(No argument is ever presented for this. It seems implausible on its face. I will say more about it later.)

Step 3. Assumption: The sentence: (a) "Snow is white" is logically equivalent to the sentence: (b) "The unique x such that (x is identical with Diogenes) is identical with the unique x such that (x is identical with Diogenes and snow is white)."

("Logical equivalence" is a technical term. Two statements are logically equivalent iff they have the same truth value in every model. On this definition there exists a semantics for definite descriptions according to which (a) and (b) are logically equivalent.)

Step 4. Assumption: The sentence: "Grass is green" is logically equivalent to the sentence: "The unique x such that (x is identical with Diogenes) is identical with the unique x such that (x is identical with Diogenes and grass is green)."

(This is just like assumption 3. The same considerations apply.)

Step 5. Assumption: The expression "the unique x such that (x is identical with Diogenes and snow is white)" refers to the same object as the expression "the unique x such that (x is identical with Diogenes and grass is green)."

Now given these assumptions, from step 1 we can derive

Step 6. The statement that snow is white corresponds to the fact that the unique x such that (x is identical with Diogenes) is

identical with the unique x such that (x is identical with Diogenes
and snow is white).

(This is derived by the principle stated in step 2b allowing substitutability of logically equivalent sentences and the assumption
stated in step 3 that the two sentences are logically equivalent.)

And from step 6, by the principle of substitutability of coreferring expressions stated in 2a together with the coreference stated
in 5, we get

Step 7. The statement that snow is white corresponds to the fact
that the unique x such that (x is identical with Diogenes) is
identical with the unique x such that (x is identical with Diogenes
and grass is green).

But now we just go backward, substituting the logical equivalence
stated in Step 4, and once again employing the principle stated in
2b, we get

Step 8. The statement that snow is white corresponds to the fact
that grass is green.

But this result would show that for any two true statements, the
first corresponds to the fact stated by the second. Any two true
statements can be stuck in for "Snow is white" and "Grass is green"
to show that any true statement corresponds to any and all facts.
Therefore the notion of correspondence is empty and the correspondence theory of truth has been refuted.

What are we to make of this argument? I think it is implausible
and the most that such an argument shows is the falsity of its presuppositions.[15] In this case, it seems to me the most the argument
could show is the falsity of assumption 2b, that logically equivalent
sentences can be substituted *salva veritate* in contexts such as Step
1. Quite apart from this example, 2b has counterintuitive consequences. For example, according to 2b, from the fact that the
statement that (snow is white) corresponds to the fact that (snow
is white), it follows that the statement that (snow is white) corre-

sponds to the fact that (snow is white and 2 + 2 = 4)! In the sling-shot argument, the first derived step, 6, is false since the statement that snow is white corresponds to no facts about Diogenes. Diogenes and his identity are quite irrelevant where the fact that snow is white is concerned. In simple terms, from the true statement that

1. The statement that snow is white corresponds to the fact that snow is white ,

we cannot validly derive

6. The statement that snow is white corresponds to the fact that the unique x such that (x is identical with Diogenes) is identical with the unique x such that (x is identical with Diogenes and snow is white).

But, someone might object, isn't this just begging the question? After all, precisely the point at issue is whether or not the correspondence theory has unwanted logical consequences, so we cannot just reject the alleged consequences out of hand. The answer to this objection is given by the account of facts, as well as of truth and correspondence that I gave in Chapter 9. In spite of their great generality, these are humble, ordinary words and their ordinary use has to be respected in any philosophical account that relies on that use. I have argued that the whole notion of "fact" that is relevant to this discussion is the notion of something that *makes a statement true or in virtue of which it is true.* If I am right about that, then any set of logical constraints such as assumption 2b on sentential contexts such as step 1 has to respect these features of the meaning of "fact," as well as the intuitive features of "true" and "correspond." On our ordinary intuitive conception, the truth maker for the statement that snow is white is the fact that snow is white. It is, I believe, obvious that the self-identity of Diogenes (or the fact that 2 + 2 = 4) has nothing whatever to do with what makes the statement that snow is white true. In short, it is a condition of adequacy on any account of truth and correspondence that it must respect the intuitive notions of "fact," "truth," and "correspondence." The slingshot argument precisely fails to do that because it accepts a principle, 2b, which runs counter to the ordinary intuitive notions.

The charge of begging the question is subject to *tu quoque.* It begs the question against the correspondence theory to assume that it is subject to principles like 2b, when no argument is given for assuming that 2b is applicable. Why should we suppose that sentences like 1 permit truth-preserving substitutions of logically equivalent sentences, when such substitutions give immediately counterintuitive results? Any principle that violates our intuitions would require a great deal of argument for its justification, and in this case no justification at all is offered for counterintuitive results.

Another way to put this point is simply to note that *identity of facts* is not preserved under substitutability of logically equivalent sentences; and the sentence form

"The statement that a corresponds to the fact that b"

permits truth-preserving substitution on the right-hand side of "corresponds to" of noun phrases of the form "the fact that c" only in cases where

The fact that b is identical with the fact that c.

But intuitively that condition is not preserved by the Diogenes example. Intuitively, the fact that snow is white *is not the same fact* as the fact that the unique x such that (x is identical with Diogenes) is identical with the unique x such that (x is identical with Diogenes and snow is white). And if we had any doubts about our intuition, the obviously counterintuitive nature of 6 should be sufficient to remove them. Since 1 is true and 6 is false, it follows that the inference is invalid. From true premises only true conclusions can be validly derived.

It is important to point out that the problem is not with the apparent nonextensionality of "X corresponds to Y." That context is completely extensional with respect to substitutability of corefer-ring expressions for "X" and "Y." The problem is with the nonex-tensionalitiy of the expression "the fact that b." That expression does not preserve sameness of reference under substitution of logically equivalent sentences. But why should it? Why should facts about snow be identical with, be the very same facts as, facts about Diogenes or anybody else? Where the fact that snow is white is concerned, Diogenes has nothing to do with it. Intuitively the idea that those two facts are really the same seems out of the question.

I conclude that the slingshot argument does not refute the cor-respondence theory.

Conclusion

One way to get at the underlying thrust of what I have been arguing in this book is this: On my view the traditional opposition that
we tend to make between biology and culture is as misguided as
the traditional opposition between body and mind. Just as mental
states are higher-level features of our nervous system, and consequently there is no opposition between the mental and the physical, the mental is simply a set of physical features of the brain at a
higher level of description than that of neurons; so there is no opposition between culture and biology; culture is the form that biology takes. There could not be an opposition between culture
and biology, because if there were, biology would always win. Different cultures are different forms that an underlying biological
substructure can be manifested in. But if that is right, then there
ought to be a more or less continuous story that goes from an ontology of biology to an ontology that includes cultural and institutional forms; there should not be any radical break. The thesis I
have been arguing is that there is no radical break. The connect-

ing terms between biology and culture are, not surprisingly, consciousness and intentionality. What is special about culture is the manifestation of collective intentionality and, in particular, the collective assignment of functions to phenomena where the function cannot be performed solely in virtue of the sheer physical features of the phenomena. From dollar bills to cathedrals, and from football games to nation-states, we are constantly encountering new social facts where the facts exceed the physical features of the underlying physical reality.

However, though there is a continuum from the chemistry of neurotransmitters such as seretonin and norepinephrine to the content of such mental states as believing that Proust is a better novelist than Balzac, mental states are distinguished from other physical phenomena in that they are either conscious or potentially so. Where there is no accessibility to consciousness, at least in principle, there are no mental states. Similarly, though there is a continuity in collective behavior between lions attacking a hyena and the Supreme Court making a constitutional decision, institutional structures have a special feature, namely, symbolism. The biological capacity to make something symbolize—or mean, or express—something beyond itself is the basic capacity that underlies not only language but all other forms of institutional reality as well. Language is itself an institutional structure because it involves the imposition of a special kind of function on brute physical entities that have no natural relation to that function. Certain sorts of sounds or marks *count as* words and sentences, and certain sorts of utterances *count as* speech acts. The agentive function is that of *representing*, in one or other of the possible speech act modes, objects and states of affairs in the world. Agents who can do this collectively have the fundamental precondition of all other institutional structures: Money, property, marriage, government, and universities all exist by forms of human agreement that essentially involve the capacity to symbolize.

Endnotes

Chapter 1. The Building Blocks of Social Reality

1. J. R. Searle, "What Is a Speech Act," in Black, Max ed. *Philosophy in America* (Ithaca, N.Y.: Cornell University Press, London: Allen N. Unwin, 1965); and J. R. Searle, *Speech Acts, An essay in the Philosophy of Language,* (New York: Cambridge University Press, 1969) The notion of "brute fact" in this sense is due to G.E.M. Anscombe, "On Brute Facts," *Analysis* 18, no. 3 (1958).
2. For an argument for the last two claims, i.e., that the notion of deep unconscious rule following is incoherent and that computation is observer-relative, see John R. Searle, *The Rediscovery of the Mind* (Cambridge, Mass., London: MIT Press, 1992), chaps. 7 and 9, respectively.
3. L. Wright, "Functions" in *The Philosophical Review* 82, no. 2 (April 1973), 137–68. See also P. Achinstein, "Functional Explanation" in *The Nature of Explanation* (New York: Oxford University Press 1983), pp. 263–90.

4. The use of these terms to describe the distinction was originally suggested to me by Jennifer Hudin.

5. For an explanation of the sort of imposition of intentionality involved in meaning, see Searle, *Intentionality, An Essay in the Philosophy of Mind,* especially chap. 6.

6. I discuss some of these in John R. Searle, "Collective Intentions and Actions," in *Intentions in Communication,* P. Cohen, J. Morgan, and M. E. Pollack, eds. Cambridge, Mass.: Bradford Books, MIT Press, 1990).

7. I do not wish to suggest that my views are uncontroversial or unchallenged. There are several other powerful conceptions of collective intentionality. See especially M. Gilbert, *On Social Facts* (London: Routledge, 1989); M. Bratman, "Shared Cooperative Activity," *Philosophical Review* 101, no. 2 (1992), 327–41; and R. Tuomela and K. Miller, "We-intentions," *Philosophical Studies* 53 (1988), 367–89.

8. Searle, *Speech Acts.*

9. A related distinction was introduced by J. Rawls, "Two Concepts of Rules," *Philosophical Review* 64 (1955).

10. E.g., Anthony Giddens, *The Constitution of Society: Outline of the Theory of Structuration* (Berkeley: University of California Press, 1984), pp. 19ff.

Chapter 2. Creating Institutional Facts

1. John R. Searle, *Expression and Meaning: Studies in the Theory of Speech Acts* (Cambridge and New York: Cambridge University Press, 1979), chap. 1.

2. I attempt to explain the relationship between the individual component and the collective component of collective intentionality in John R. Searle, "Collective Intentions and Actions," in *Intentions in Communication,* P. Cohen, J. Morgan, and M. E. Pollack, eds. (Cambridge, Mass: Bradford Books, MIT Press, 1990).

3. The classic text is W. Koehler, *The Mentality of Apes,* 2d ed. (London: Kegan Paul, Trench and Trubner, 1927).

More recently, E. O. Wilson writes, "Tool using occurs sporadically among the species of higher primates, mostly to a degree no greater than in other vertebrate groups. However the chimpanzee has a repertory so rich and sophisticated that the species stands qualitatively above all other animals and well up the scale toward man." *Sociobiology: The New Synthesis* (Cambridge, Mass.: Harvard University Press, 1975), p. 73.

4. Werner Kummer, *Primate Societies* (Chicago: Aldine, 1971), p. 118.
5. This situation, by the way, still exists with British currency. On the British twenty pound note it says, "I promise to pay the bearer on demand the sum of twenty pounds." It is signed by the chief cashier of the Bank of England.
6. I will use the expressions "X term," "Y term," and "C term" to refer indifferently either to the actual *entities* that are the values of these three variables or to the verbal expressions that we substitute for the expressions "X," "Y," and "C." I realize that there is always a danger of a use-mention confusion, but I believe the context will make it clear whether I am referring to an expression or to an entity referred to by that expression. In cases where there might be a confusion, I will make the distinction explicit by using, for example, the distinction between "the X expression" and "the X element." The first of these will refer to an expression; the second will refer to an actual entity.

Chapter 3. Language and Social Reality

1. Donald M. Broom, *The Biology of Behavior: Mechanisms, Functions and Applications* (Cambridge: Cambridge University Press, 1981), p. 196–197

Chapter 4: The General Theory of Institutional Facts Part I: Iteration, Interaction, and Logical Structure

1. For extended further discussion see John R. Searle, *Speech Acts: An Essay in the Philosophy of Language* (Cambridge: Cambridge

University Press, 1969), and John R. Searle, *Expression and Meaning: Studies in the Theory of Speech Acts* (Cambridge: Cambridge University Press, 1979).

Chapter 6. Background Abilities and the Explanation of Social Phenomena

1. N. Chomsky, *Reflections on Language* (New York: Pantheon, 1975).
2. J. A. Fodor, *The Language of Thought* (New York: Crowell, 1975).
3. For further discussion, see John R. Searle, *The Rediscovery of the Mind,* (Cambridge, Mass.: MIT Press, Cambridge MA and London, 1992), chap. 7.
4. John R. Searle, *Intentionality: An Essay in the Philosophy of Mind* (New York: Cambridge University Press, 1983), and op. cit. supra.
5. Searle, *The Rediscovery of the Mind,* chap. 7.
6. The example, I believe, is originally due to Robyn Carston, "Implicature, Explicature and Truth-Theoretic Semantics," in S. Davis, ed., *Pragmatics: A Reader* (Oxford: Oxford University Press, 1991), pp. 33–51.
7. Ludwig Wittgenstein, *Philosophical Investigations* (Oxford: Basil Blackwell, 1953), part II, sec. xi.
8. Ibid., part I, para. 201.
9. Ibid., Part I, para. 324ff and passim.
10. Daniel Dennett, *The Intentional Stance* (Cambridge, Mass.: MIT Press, 1987).

Chapter 7. Does the Real World Exist?
Part I: Attacks on Realism

1. An example of a realist philosopher who rejects the correspondence theory is Peter Strawson. See his "Truth" *Proceedings of the Aristotelian Society,* supplementary volume 24 (1950).
2. H. Putnam, *Realism With a Human Face* (Cambridge, Mass.: Harvard University Press, 1990), p. 23.

3. Quoted by N. Goodman, *Of Mind and Other Matters* (Cambridge, Mass.: Harvard University Press, 1984), p. 36.

4. H. R. Maturana, F. J. Varela, *Autopoiesis and Cognition, The Realization of the Living* (Dordrecht: D. Reidel, 1980).

5. Terry Winograd, "Three Responses to Situation Theory," *Center for the Study of Language and Information*, Report No. CSLI-87-106, 1987, and Terry Winograd and Fernando Flores, *Understanding Computers and Cognition* (Norewood, N.J.: Ablex, 1986), chap. 5.

6. G. Levine, "Looking for the Real: Epistemology in Science and Culture," in G. Levine, ed., *Realism and Representation: Essays on the Problem of Realism in Relation to Science, Literature and Culture,* (Madison: University of Wisconsin Press, 1993), p. 13.

7. J. Derrida, *Limited Inc.* (Evanston, Ill.: Northwestern University Press, 1988), p. 136.

8. Putnam, *Realism with a Human Face,* p. 96ff. H. Putnam, *The Many Faces of Realism* (LaSalle, Ill.: Open Court, 1987), p. 18ff.

9. N. Goodman, *Of Mind and Other Matters,* p. 36.

10. Putnam, *Reason, Truth and History* (Cambridge: Cambridge University Press, 1981), p. xi. The phrase is repeated in *The Many Faces of Realism,* p. 1.

11. Ludwig Wittgenstein, *Philosophical Investigations,* (Oxford: Basil Blackwell, 1953), part.1, para. 464 (my translation).

12. I apologize for the brevity of this discussion. I have discussed these same issues in greater detail in chap. 2 of *Intentionality.* For the best argument against the sense datum theory, see J. L. Austin, *Sense and Sensibilia* (New York: Oxford University Press, 1962).

13. Ludwig Wittgenstein, *Tractatus Logico-Philosophicus* (London: Routledge and Kegan Paul, 1922).

14. Putnam, attacking realism, describes it as the view that "*Truth* is supposed to be *radically nonepistemic.*" *Meaning and the Moral Sciences,* London: Routledge & Kegan Paul, 1978, p. 125. But realism is the claim that *reality* is radically nonepistemic. And if it

should turn out that the concept of "truth" is not radically nonepistemic, then we should simply have to get another concept that was, for we need a nonepistemic term to describe the correspondence between our statements and the radically non-epistemic real world.

Chapter 8. Does the Real World Exist?
Part II: Could There Be a Proof of External Realism?

1. I have to say "in general" because, for example, some statements are self-referential, e.g., "This sentence is in English."
2. It is related to, but not the same as, Tarski's Convention T. See Alfred Tarski, "Der Wahrheitsbegriff in den formalisierten Sprachen," *Studia Philosophica* (1935) 261–405; translated as "The Concept of Truth in Formalized Languages" in Alfred Tarski, *Logic, Semantics, Metamathematics* (Oxford: Clarendon Press, 1956).
3. J. L. Austin, "Truth," and P. F. Strawson, "Truth," *Proceedings of the Aristotelian Society* 34 (1950). Reprinted in Pitcher, ed., *Truth* (Englewood Cliffs: N.J.: Prentice Hall, 1964).
4. Strawson, in Pitcher, *Truth*, p. 32.
5. Ibid., p. 40, italics in the original.
6. Ludwig Wittgenstein, *Tractatus Logico-Philosophicus* (London: Routledge and Kegan Paul, 1922).
7. Strawson, in Pitcher, *Truth*, p. 38.
8. op. cit., p. 41
9. "What is a fact? A fact is a thought that is true." Gottlob Frege, "The Thought," in. P. F. Strawson, ed., *Philosophical Logic* (Oxford: Oxford University Press, 1967), p. 35.
10. Strawson, in Pitcher, *Truth*, p. 38.
11. Such statements can no doubt be paraphrased in ways that do not mention facts, but that is beside the point. The point here is that they make sense in a way that attributing causal powers to statements does not.
12. For examples of these views, see F. P. Ramsey, "Facts and Proposi-

tions," *Proceedings of the Aristotelian Society* supp. vol. 7 (1927), reprinted in Pitcher, ed., *Truth;* P. Horwich, *Truth* (Oxford: Basil Blackwell, 1990), and W.V.O. Quine, *Pursuit of Truth,* rev. ed. (Cambridge, Mass.: Harvard University Press, 1992).

13. For more on this distinction, see J. R. Searle, *Intentionality* (Cambridge and New York: Cambridge University Press, 1983), p. 13.

14. Here is the entire argument as stated by Davidson:

> The principles are these: if a statement corresponds to the fact described by an expression of the form 'the fact that p', then it corresponds to the fact described by 'the fact that q' provided either (1) the sentences that replace 'p' and 'q' are logically equivalent, or (2) 'p' differs from 'q' only in that a singular term has been replaced by a coextensive singular term. The confirming argument is this. Let 's' abbreviate some true sentence. Then surely the statement that s corresponds to the fact that s. But we may substitute for the second 's' the logically equivalent '(the x such that x is identical with Diogenes and s) is identical with (the x such that x is identical with Diogenes)'. Applying the principle that we may substitute coextensive singular terms, we can substitute 't' for 's' in the last quoted sentence, provided 't' is true. Finally, reversing the first step we conclude that the statement that s corresponds to the fact that t, where 's' and 't' are any true sentences.

Inquiries into Truth and Interpretation (Oxford: Clarendon Press, 1984), p. 42.

15. There are a number of criticisms of the slingshot argument. I believe the one closest in spirit to mine is in J. Barwise and J. Perry, *Situations and Attitudes* (Cambridge, Mass.: MIT Press, 1983).

Name Index

Subject Index